REDEFINING SPORTS MEDIA

This book argues that the examination of sports media within cultural and media studies is organized around more than just a shared topic: mediated sports.

What count as "sports media" in journals, books, and conferences are extremely diverse; they can cover athlete expression on social media, shoe commercials, gender in sports commentary, Indigenous name change activists, and fantasy sports. Besides being mediated and, in some cases, loosely connected to sports events and leagues, it is hard to see what they all share that could serve as the foundation for a unified field of study. Jason Kido Lopez argues that sports media are defined by genre, which is reflected in their industries, within their content, and by their audiences. Throughout the media and cultural complex, sports and sports media are built on the genre of live and real competition and, therefore, to study sports media is to study that genre. Each chapter will explore how the genre is constructed in commodification of mediated sport, representation within sports media, athlete expression, sports fandom, and gaming around sports.

This book will be of interest to those studying sports media and media and cultural studies, but also can be used as an introductory survey of the research on sports media from a media and cultural studies perspective.

Jason Kido Lopez is an assistant professor in the Department of Communication Arts at the University of Wisconsin-Madison. His work on sports media focuses on athlete activism and games based on sports like fantasy sports and sports betting.

REDEFINING SPORTS MEDIA

Jason Kido Lopez

NEW YORK AND LONDON

Designed cover image: elenabs/Getty Images

First published 2023
by Routledge
605 Third Avenue, New York, NY 10158

and by Routledge
4 Park Square, Milton Park, Abingdon, Oxon, OX14 4RN

Routledge is an imprint of the Taylor & Francis Group, an informa business

© 2023 Jason Kido Lopez

The right of Jason Kido Lopez to be identified as author of this work has been asserted in accordance with sections 77 and 78 of the Copyright, Designs and Patents Act 1988.

All rights reserved. No part of this book may be reprinted or reproduced or utilised in any form or by any electronic, mechanical, or other means, now known or hereafter invented, including photocopying and recording, or in any information storage or retrieval system, without permission in writing from the publishers.

Trademark notice: Product or corporate names may be trademarks or registered trademarks, and are used only for identification and explanation without intent to infringe.

Library of Congress Cataloging-in-Publication Data
Names: Lopez, Jason Kido, author.
Title: Redefining sports media / Jason Kido Lopez.
Description: New York, N.Y. : Routledge, 2023. | Includes bibliographical references and index.
Identifiers: LCCN 2022055619 (print) | LCCN 2022055620 (ebook) | ISBN 9780367751272 (paperback) | ISBN 9780367758516 (hardback) | ISBN 9781003164272 (ebook)
Subjects: LCSH: Mass media and sports. | Sports journalism.
Classification: LCC GV742 .L67 2023 (print) | LCC GV742 (ebook) | DDC 070.4/49796—dc23/eng/20221121
LC record available at https://lccn.loc.gov/2022055619
LC ebook record available at https://lccn.loc.gov/2022055620

ISBN: 978-0-367-75851-6 (hbk)
ISBN: 978-0-367-75127-2 (pbk)
ISBN: 978-1-003-16427-2 (ebk)

DOI: 10.4324/9781003164272

Typeset in Bembo
by Apex CoVantage, LLC

*For my mom, the only person who has read everything
Lori and I have written*

CONTENTS

Acknowledgments   *viii*

Introduction: Sports Media, Genre, and Live and Real Competition   1

1   Branding Live and Real Competition   14

2   Representing Live and Real Competition   37

3   Live and Real Athlete Expression   58

4   Fans of Live and Real Competition   74

5   Games Based on Live and Real Competition   90

Conclusion: The Pervasiveness of Live and Real Competition   111

Index   *123*

ACKNOWLEDGMENTS

In 2012, my wife, Lori, and I made a decision. I recently received my PhD and she was about to earn hers, so we'd both go on the market and the other would follow whoever got the best job. Lori was offered a tenure-track job in the Department of Communication Arts at the University of Wisconsin-Madison (UW) and we never hesitated. In Madison, I was lucky to find work teaching at Madison College, teaching with UW's Integrated Liberal Studies program and eventually teaching a few classes in the Philosophy Department. However, I ultimately ended up finding a home in Communication Arts along with Lori. Over the course of years, I moved from researching self-deception and philosophy of mind to sports media—a jump that I never would have been able to make without a lot of help.

I, first of all, wouldn't be writing this if hadn't started down the academic path by people at Pomona College and Indiana University. Professors Brian Keeley and Jay Atlas all prepared me for graduate school, and Jonathan Weinberg, Colin Allen, and Timothy O'Connor guided me through the process. I need to mention especially Paul Spade, who was my dissertation advisor but did so much more for me. Paul taught me about academic curiosity and about finding questions that were interesting to me. Our chats at Nicks over a pound or two about Kierkegaard and Sartre helped me develop as a scholar but also got me excited about being in graduate school. I should also mention my fellow Indiana University graduate students. To those of you who were further along in your studies when I arrived—Josh Alexander, Mark Wilson, Dan Kirchner, Tony Aumann, Jeremy McCrary, and Justin Brown—I looked up to your intellectual rigor and, for some of you, your dart-playing and wiffle ball skills. I want to thank especially my roomie, Kari Theurer, for being my go-to for all the important things: philosophy of mind, burritos, cocktails, and proper nest-making. All of you made grad school so much fun.

I also want to thank those of you who gave me a home before Madison, UW, and Comm Arts. Thanks to the Annenberg Homies—George Villanueva, Beth Boser, Brandon Anderson, Allie Noyes, Garrett Broad, and Evan Brody—for being so welcoming to me when Lori was a grad student at the University of Southern California. It has been great to keep up through all the sports gaming and, now, through seeing you at the occasional conference. Thanks to Siena College's Philosophy Department, Josh Alexander, and Jennifer McErlean for your support when I was a post doc. I also am extremely appreciative of UW's Integrated Liberal Studies program for giving me a place to teach topics I was passionate about to dedicated and interested students. I hope to connect with you all again soon.

Part of feeling welcome writing and thinking about sports media came from those of you who I met at conferences, particularly the Society for Cinema and Media Studies and the International Communication Association. Thanks to you all for making me feel so comfortable in new surroundings. I'd like to mention Evan Brody again, for being a great friend and someone who has been extremely supportive of my switch to thinking about sports media. I don't know how far my interest in sports media would have gone without you. You have made me feel as comfortable in a new field as a good pair of pa-jam-as.

Thanks to Routledge and Emma Sherriff for reaching out about this project and helping to shape it. It started as more of an introductory book, and you helped me see its argument. I also want to thank Andrew Schrock at Indelible Voice for his work on this manuscript. You were a pleasure to collaborate with and this book is much better due to your help.

This book would literally not exist without the people of the UW's Department of Communication Arts. As a group, you all supported me in finding the topic of sports media in the first place and then in pursuing that interest. From giving me opportunities to teach, to helping me attend conferences, to supporting my writing, the department has made me feel as though my niche focus on sports was valuable and that I was worthy of being included with you amazing people.

Thanks particularly to Mike Xenos, who was chair of the department during my shift to studying sports. I can't express how meaningful his dedication to helping me find an academic home is to me. I know I wouldn't be here doing something I love without your efforts. Thanks also to Jennell Johnson for sharing your insights as a faculty mentor. I'd also like to mention Jeff Smith for making me feel so at home in the hallways of Vilas Hall. Our conversations—that usually involve you celebrating good fantasy football picks and me lamenting mine—really made me feel at home and I enjoy them every time we cross paths. Also, to the Real Real Executive Committee of Comm Arts—Allison Prasch, Darshana Mini, Anirban Baishya, and Lillie Williamson—it has been great to go through assistant professor life with colleagues as supportive as you all. I'd also like to thank Lille for taking the time to chat with me every week—rain, shine, or even snow. Additionally, I'd like to mention Eric Hoyt, who has always given great advice and been an advocate for me, usually with a solid sports metaphor thrown in for good measure. Finally, I want to thank the past and present graduate students of the Comm Arts Department. In the early years, you made the odd philosopher feel at home among you all and, more recently, have supported my teaching and research. I'd like to especially mention Austin Morris, Jacob Mertens, Taylore Woodhouse, and Will Quade for all your thoughtful discussion about sports media. I have learned from you all and, therefore, you have all shaped this book.

Before I taught even one class in Communication Arts, I was lucky enough to be immediately accepted by what has become some of my best friends and their families. I cannot state how thankful I am to Jeremy Morris, Derek Johnson, and Jonathan Gray for making me feel as though I was unquestionably one of you. Despite the fact that you three and Lori had so much to talk about—the university, the department, the Media, and Cultural Studies area—you always took the time to make me feel included. It is hard for me to give an accurate picture of all of the support and advocating you did for me, and I'm sure I don't even know all of it. However, I know for a fact that I wouldn't be in a position to write something like this without you three helping me every step of the way. Thanks Jer (Office Buddy), Derek (Hand of the King/Admiral), and Jonathan (Corey Hart) for all the innumerable things you've done to make sure that Lori and I had a home here in Madison. I also want to mention, along with Jonathan, the rest of Podfam: Monica Grant and Abby Gray. From freezing on a porch, to hiding in a basement, to huddling around a game board, seeing you every week was one of the few good things to come out of the pandemic.

I'd like to end by thanking my family. To the DesRochers family—and Doug and Sharlene in particular—thanks so much for your support. I couldn't ask for better in-laws, and I'm sorry that I didn't work any Oregon Ducks references into this book. To my parents, Anthony and Donna Lopez, I'm so thankful for everything you have done for me. I'm sorry we live so far away, but you know that my favorite trips are those in which I get to see you—especially in Vegas. Mom, thanks for reading all my writing, even if it is analytic philosophy. Dad, thanks for always being on-call for a sports chat.

Finally, thanks most of all to Lori. You have been part of every step of this process. I'm so amazed that we now get to live a life where we get to work, WoD, eat, play, watch TV, and cuddle Boba together. I'm so, so lucky to be able to share all of this with you and I couldn't have done it without you.

INTRODUCTION

Sports Media, Genre, and Live and Real Competition

Spectrum SportsNet LA broadcasts a Los Angeles Dodgers' victory over the San Francisco Giants throughout Southern California. Nike debuts a commercial advertising LeBron James's newest shoes. ESPN releases a ten-part documentary about Michael Jordan's career with the Chicago Bulls. DraftKings offers a million-dollar prize for the winner of a daily fantasy football contest. Fans log into LoLSports.com to watch the *League of Legends* (*LoL*) esport. The National Football League (NFL) announces a policy that players must not kneel for the national anthem. The *Washington Post* publishes an article on the economic consequences of legalizing sports betting. Antonio Brown attacks the NFL on Instagram after being removed from the league due to sexual assault allegations. A young fan plays as the US Women's National Team (USWNT) on EA Sports' popular soccer video game, *FIFA*.

Sports media are incredibly diverse, which means media and cultural studies' interdisciplinarity is particularly well suited to study them. The previously mentioned events raise their own questions about sports media, which can be answered with media and cultural studies' distinct theories and methods. An analysis of the representation of James in his commercials is very different from a study of how fandom of the USWNT is expressed through gaming, for instance. Researchers like Walter Gantz (2014) think that there can be "no single talk, annual conference, book, journal, grand theory or applied method [that] can fully capture the scope of the descriptive and theory-based work" on sports media (p. 7). For this reason, the theoretical and methodological heterogeneity of media and cultural studies helps examine the variety of sports media topics and objects. Indeed, "[m]uch of the writing on sport and the media addresses general issues within media studies" (Bernstein & Blain, 2002, p. 1). The field of media and cultural studies and sports media are well suited for each other.

DOI: 10.4324/9781003164272-1

Drawing on this literature, this book will argue that the study of sports media is uniquely situated within media and cultural studies. With its diversity and inability to be contained by one theory or method, sports media occupies a distinctive space that justifies its place within the broader field. The study of sports media is also organized around more than just a topic—it isn't simply the study of sports when they are mediated. However, the connection of media to sports should be taken seriously. But what are sports?

We could define sports analytically. For example, Bernard Suits (1988) defines sport as the competitive use of physical skills. There are some merits to his definition, as it seems intuitive that sports involve rules of play in which winners and losers are determined (competition). Those rules determine the relevant abilities needed to compete (skills), which are athletic in nature (physical). However, as with all concepts defined in this way, counterexamples loom. A quick survey of broadcasts on channels like ESPN, NBC Sports, and Fox Sports reveals deviations. Does Nathan's Hot Dog Eating Contest involve physical skills? What about a National Association for Stock Car Auto Racing (NASCAR) race or a bowling tournament organized by the Professional Bowlers Association? Does drone racing or esports count? There are even sports that violate the competition condition, as World Wrestling Entertainment (WWE) matches are semi-planned performances. Although Suits's definition is restrictive, such questions are helpful to orient us around shared expectations of how sports are defined and mediated.

First, we might disagree with some particularities of Suits's conception of sport, but his general conception of sport carries some weight. Sport does indeed carry *some* expectation of a physical, skill-based competition. Second, interpersonal debates about what counts as a sport are common among sports fans and are had in stadia, bars, and living rooms. Therefore, what counts as sports are constantly being formed and contested. Third, we've seen earlier how sports are defined through media; what sports media companies choose to cover and how they cover it inform the shared public understanding of sport. Sports carry with them a loose set of expectations, which are partially debated and worked out through media. These mediated debates suggest that what counts as sport is formed culturally and therefore is worthy of a cultural analysis which recognizes that "sports forms (practices, products, institutions, etc.) can only be understood by the way that they are articulated into a particular set of complex social, economic, political, and technological relationships that compose the social context" (Andrews & Giardina, 2008, p. 406). Sports, therefore, are difficult to define because they are a cultural category constantly under construction.

Strong opinions about what sports are emerge from how deeply sports are tied into US culture. Many of us grew up with physical education from elementary school through high school, and even in college. Though there are other parts to physical education, playing sports is a shared component. Sports are also played as recreation, and teams and leagues are organized for children and adults alike.

Public spaces are dedicated to sports. For a select few athletes, sports become a high-level competition that gets increasingly professionalized as they get older. Eventually, it leads some to monetary compensation. Furthermore, many people watch sport in person, as families and friends might attend a recreational sporting event. Of course, thousands of people can congregate to watch professional, collegiate, and even high school sports in person. Finally, and most saliently, people engage with sport through media. Sports and media have become fused together in "mediasport" (Wenner, 1998). Furthermore, sports media has merged with popular culture. Sports celebrities are covered in gossip outlets and sports are some of the most popular video games. Sports are now reported on in major news sources and can be found on TVs in non-sports-themed restaurants. Culture and sports media aren't separate entities but intertwined in a *complex* (Rowe, 2004; Jhally, 1989). This media/culture complex keeps sports constantly around us and is where the concept of sport is perpetually being shaped.

Suits's work and definitional debates about sports demonstrate that the study of sports media is more than the study of sports when they are mediated. There is no settled definition of sport upon which to build a field of investigation, and sports media extends well beyond athletic competition. Those who analyze sports media, as we saw earlier, can research video games, social media, journalism, sponsorship deals, and documentaries. Such media diversity is reflected in consumption by sports fans, as Andrew Billings (2014) notes, since "a person can consume sports media for hours each day without ever seeing or hearing a sporting event" (p. 184). There are signs in what we've seen earlier that the relationship between media and sports opens diverse topics and research opportunities. So what is sports media?

Because *sport* comes with certain expectations that are shaped by the media/culture complex, I argue that it is fruitful to think of it as a media genre. Jason Mittell (2004) conceptualizes sports as a genre in his broader work on television genre. He points out that sports form a television genre like soap operas, reality TV, and game shows. Mittell argues that genre is built by more than just text, since it is impossible to distill genres completely. His book begins with a question about another genre of television: Does a sitcom need to be a half hour long? His question should be reminiscent of the questions we asked earlier: Are eating hot dogs or scripted wrestling sports? We might have different intuitions about what counts as a sport or soap opera based on the texts. So for Mittell (2017), "[g]enre categories do not simply emerge from the texts that they categorize, but rather are created, debated, refashioned, and dismissed in various cultural sites" (p. 81). We already saw this earlier for sport; how it is conceived is worked out interpersonally, institutionally, and through media.

The genre of sport is formed throughout the complex of sports, media, and culture. Mittell (2004) offers a TV-specific account of genre and argues that television genre is different enough from film and literature that it needs its own description. For example, television has to account for scheduling, unlike film or literature. Mittell's view could be applied to the genre of sport on television and used to explore how sport is constructed around and through cable sports channels like ESPN and FS1. However, these channels' constructions of sports are—as with sports media more broadly—so much more than a television genre. The genre is also formed through print, radio, websites, social media, games, and billboards. Given the increasing role that the digital plays in mediasport, it is worthwhile to give special consideration to "identifying features of the marketplace, communications technology, and uses of media that explain the appearance and operation of media sport in the digital age" (Hutchins & Rowe, 2012, p. 5). Even though television has a crucial relationship to sport, to make television primary would be a mistake since sport is a transmedia genre.

Mittell's insights about television relate to how the genre of sports can be created across media. Looking beyond the text, Mittell (2017) argues that *generic categories* gather "a cluster of assumptions and practices that connect to its presumed cultural significance, viewership, aesthetic value, and industrial strategies" (p. 83). I believe that the transmedia genre of sports is no different, as it too is constructed by sports and media companies, diverse sports texts, and sports fans. In this book, we will explore how the genre of sport is expected, constructed, debated, and sold throughout mediasport and the wider sport and culture/media complex. As with the study of sports media generally, we can analyze how the genre is expressed throughout the "communicative chain [of] production, message and reception" (Whannel, 2000). Indeed, the generic expectations of sport are throughout sports media and can be branded and sold by companies and individuals. It can be infused into narratives and storylines, and expected and enjoyed by audiences.

The transmedia sports genre is broad enough to account for the diversity of sports, sports media, and their academic study. The generic conventions of sport can be expressed in many ways and for this reason media and cultural studies' interdisciplinarity remains an analytic strength. The genre, however, marks a site at which diverse research on sports media can find common ground. I will argue that the study of sports media has always been about genre and, once we make that explicit, it does important work for the future of the field of study. Foregrounding genre reframes and refocuses the field, giving researchers avenues to reorganize and resituate disparate topics, research methods, and theoretical commitments.

The remainder of this introduction will be dedicated to explaining what it means to study the genre of sports from the media and cultural studies' perspective. The following chapters will argue that the genre is found throughout sports media, as demonstrated through specific sites that anchor our discussion. Since a survey of the entire field is impossible, I have chosen five sites to explore: how the genre is commodified industrially; is represented in sports texts; shapes athlete expression; informs fan engagement; and is the basis for sports-based games like fantasy sports, sports betting, and video games. Using the lens of genre on these five topics will help envision a field of study (re)formed.

The Genre of Sports: Live and Real Competition

The competition of sports involves epistemic uncertainty, which encompasses more than just the final score and who wins. The route to the game's end—the strategies, athletic performance, rule enforcement, and injuries—are all unknown until the event unfolds. There are, of course, parts of some sporting events that are highly probable, which only lessens epistemic uncertainty rather than dispelling it. We never know exactly what will happen in a sports competition. This tension allows for predictions during pregame shows, "hot takes" during talk shows, prognosticating stats being published online, games like fantasy and sports betting, and storytelling in film and television. Sports events are unknown because they are unscripted, unlike many other entertainment properties. Part of the competition of sport, therefore, is the expectation that it is *real*. Competition perceived as authentic can be appealing, as people will often watch and pay to watch other people to compete *live*. Large stadiums and expensive broadcast rights attest to the value of watching real competition as it occurs. The genre of sports, therefore, involves an expectation of *live and real competition*.

There are other genres, like news, reality TV, and game shows, that also retain generic expectations of liveness, realness, and/or competition. Furthermore, the borders between genres are porous, as conventions and expectations can move fluidly. Using television as an example, Michael Real (2014) notes how sports-like other genres have become, citing competitive reality TV shows like *Survivor* and *American Idol* (p. 100). He also comments that sports borrow from genres like soap operas by using themes of scandal/melodrama to create dramatic narratives (Real, 2014, p. 101). As genres become popular, they borrow what works from, and are used as inspiration for, other genres. This means liveness, realness, and competition don't exclusively belong to sports and sports media. They are, however, foregrounded uniquely in it. This book is dedicated to exploring the novel ways that the expectation of liveness and realness combine with competition to create the genre of sports.

To do so involves acknowledging that the genre of sports is a construction. Constructedness might be easier to see with other genres, but it is natural for it to be obscured for sports, hidden behind prominent and real-seeming themes of liveness and realness. Other genres might similarly thrive on epistemic uncertainty (e.g., who will win a reality TV competition, who is the murderer in a mystery, or does a principal soap character have an evil twin?), but in sports uncertainty is intimately tied to feelings of liveness and realness. That's partially because sports media is connected to sports, and some sports truly have live and real aspects. As noted earlier, we don't know how a sports competition will unfold until it gets played, and we can watch what happens live. Furthermore, there's a feeling or expectation that the events unfold in front of us synchronously, which is borrowed from watching sports events in person. When such an expectation is added to the sense that the camera never lies (Seiter, 2006), sports media seems incredibly live and real. These impressions, however, obscure the myriad of ways that the liveness, realness, and competition of sports are constructed. Take a "live" broadcast of a baseball game. The competition is transmitted on a delay. It is being broadcast through a medium—television in this case—that creates the game by balancing camera angles, sound, commentary, and commercial breaks. The competition is built by narratives from announcers, sideline reporters, and statistical information. Though certainly a live and real competition is occurring when the Dodgers are beating the Giants, what people experience at home is a composition of production decisions to elicit a feeling of live and real competition.

Due to the expectations around sports and the encouragement of those expectations by media companies, sports seem naturally live and real. Focusing on sound makes this point well. The sounds of the game contribute to feelings of liveness, realness, and competition. However, where the mics are, what they attempt to capture, and how they are mixed into the broadcast both justify and create those feelings. Furthermore, some sports broadcasts add sounds from outside of the event; bird sounds are supposedly added to coverage of The Masters golf tournament and the sounds of hooves are mixed into horse racing, for example. Even more saliently, when the German Bundesliga returned after breaking due to the COVID-19 pandemic, Fox Sports edited in crowd sounds even though the stands were empty—a practice later copied by other broadcasters of other leagues (Figure 0.1). These

FIGURE 0.1   An empty Bundesliga stadium during a game that occurred during the COVID-19 pandemic. Artificial crowd noise was played during the broadcast despite the absence of fans.

sounds were all manufactured and inserted by media companies in order to elicit the feeling that the viewer was at the event hearing the birds, horses, and other (invisible?) fans associated with the event. The feeling that one is really there renders the manufacturing of the generic markers invisible.

Because there is "no guaranteed or essential manifestation, experience, or indeed definition of sport" (Andrews & Giardina, 2008, p. 395), we will focus on how live and real competition is built within and around the sports media and culture complex. Such a focus leads to a core component of this book's argument: the generic marker of live and real competition is always at work in sports media. Sometimes, it can be at the forefront; a "live" televisual broadcast of a game—especially a mega event like the Super Bowl or World Cup Championship Game—foregrounds liveness, realness, and competition. Media companies do what they can to encourage fans' expectations of the genre. Michael Real (2014), for example, analyzes how televised broadcasts of sport fold liveness, narrative suspense, open-ended drama, and continuity into the coverage of the competition (pp. 20–23). But, as noted earlier, not everything that we'd want to count as sports media is a live broadcast, happens on television, or is a competition.

I'll suggest here, but argue with more detail in the following chapters, that liveness, realness, and competition are constantly operating in sports media. Though one might be played up more than another in a given instance, sports media regularly benefit from them because they exist in ecology in which they are so common. A Nike advertisement featuring LeBron James, for example, certainly doesn't use liveness, realness, or competition in the same way as a game broadcast. An advertisement might not even feature any basketball at all. Nike doesn't need to show James playing basketball or even wearing the shoes; it is presumed that he does so when competing on the court and in his everyday life. Furthermore, because advertisements brand companies, Nike is associated with one of the most successful basketball players of all time. Everything about James in Nike commercials depends on the assumption that he excels in live and real competition. Even in a commercial that doesn't highlight basketball, the value of James revolves around his live and real performance on the court. In the following chapters we will cover enough ground (including celebrity, branding, and commercials with more details) to make the case that to study sports media is to study the genre of live and real competition. This genre might shift over time, differ slightly across sports, and vary depending on the medium or platform, but it remains stable enough to serve as the basis for the study of sports media.

Ideology Construction Through Live and Real Competition

From a media and cultural studies perspective, it is crucial to think about how sports media and the genre of sports intersect with hegemonic power (Hargreaves & McDonald, 2000). In this book, we will approach the genre of sports as capable of creating a powerful picture of reality and normativity. The sense that sports show people, events, institutions, and ideas "as they are" makes ideologies contained within sports media seem authentic, natural, and immutable. As sports and sports media are part of and contribute to the wider cultural complex, they validate ideologies widely present in society. Hegemonic descriptions about how things are, and normative positions about how things should be, become even more justified in sport through a handful of broad presumptions about sports.

The Great Sports Myth (GSM) is the widespread "belief in the inherent purity and goodness of sport" (Coakely, 2015, p. 403). It holds that participants, consumers, and communities involved in sport all benefit from sports. When negative outcomes emerge from sport, the GSM entails that its origins are "individuals blinded by greed, fame, or an extreme desire to win as they play, coach, manage or own teams and events" (Coakely, 2015, p. 405). The GSM is a dualistic view, both descriptively and normatively. For the former, there is a difference in kind; sports are pure, while social pressures are manufactured and fake. For the latter, sports and society are evaluated differently; sports are good and social influences are bad. The GSM and generic expectation of liveness and realness operate in conjunction to validate each other. The expectation of realness from the genre can be understood as part of the purity alleged by the GSM, as winners and losers are determined through the game. Who actually has more skill or ability is demonstrated. The GSM tells us that the realness of sports is questioned only when entities outside of sports get involved. We see handwringing over threats to the purity of sports' realness all the time. Outsiders like sports bettors might try to influence the outcome of games, leading to gambling scandals. Greedy baseball players could let outside influences like fame and fortune lead them to take performance-enhancing drugs (PEDs), resulting in doping scandals. Teams in the National Basketball Association (NBA) who won't make the playoffs for a particular year might let the desire for success in future seasons drive them to lose games to get a better draft pick, causing tanking scandals. Each type of scandal undercuts the assumption of a basic pure realness to sports competitions. These cases all assume, thanks to the GSM, that there are unfortunate influences to sport from cultural and social influences. Thanks to the generic expectation of live and real competition, those cultural influences can make sports less real. Furthermore, sports that are more scripted, like WWE, are occasionally criticized for being fake (Hill, 2015), which demonstrates that realness is a desirable quality. Sports' realness, therefore, seem naturally and positively pure—a view that ignores how notions of fakery, proper audience engagement, fairness, and competition are all constructs that are established and debated throughout the culture and sports media complex. The power of the GSM is derived from its ability to render that fact invisible, making sports seem to be pure and real competition.

The idea that sports can be pure competition—along with the corollary that it is only outside entities that can pollute its purity—leads to the common trope that sports are apolitical. In other words, outside influences can affect the sanctity of competition, as we saw earlier, but they can also attack the purity of the competition by inserting foreign political meanings and symbols. The competitive use of physical skills, it is held, has nothing to do with politics. Which party one tends to vote for or what one thinks about civil rights are irrelevant when the competition starts. In fact, sports are inaccurately thought of as an opportunity to escape from these real-world concerns. Sports and sports media are rife with political messages, particularly conservative ones (Serazio, 2019, p. 277).

When political ideologies get expressed repeatedly in a space assumed to be apolitical, the ideologies themselves come to appear to be apolitical (Rowe, 2004, p. 127). We'll explore more such cases (Chapter 3), but this is the mechanism at work when athletes are told to shut up and dribble or to stick to sports. They are censured for bringing politics into the apolitical sporting realm, but they are actually bringing atypical politics into an already political realm. For example, when athletes kneel during the national anthem, they are not "making sports political," they are making their political position on police brutality and racism known during a time when normal political messages are unified in support of the US military and its actions. However, the messages about the military, as a part of the usual spectacle of American sport, adopt the appearance of being apolitical. Therefore, athlete activism seems like a political incursion into a sacred apolitical space. Regularly present ideologies are normalized and appear to be apolitical, while unusual ideologies are cast as improperly political.

If pure competition is walled off from politics and ideology, it follows that its results are determined by individual merit. Social power structures are supposedly eliminated in sport, and therefore, success in competition is the result of doing the most with what one has. Meritocracy presents another dualistic picture in which merit is based on nature and nurture. First, given that sports are pure competition and there are no outside influences on the results of the competition, then one gets what one deserves. Meritocracy carries a theme of justice; one reaps what one sows in sports. You fall short because you didn't apply yourself. If you fail to bootstrap yourself to success, it is because you didn't work hard enough. If you didn't measure up to your potential, it is your fault. Sports communicates that there are spaces in which people are in control of their fate and immune from oppressive social structures.

That success can be nurtured is bound to natural talent and ability. That is, athletes aren't capable of doing *anything* through sheer hard work; they must work with what was given to them. Part of the meritocratic picture of sports is connected with shared expectations about people's capabilities. Sports paint a picture of what types of skill, intelligence, performance, and athleticism matter and set a baseline expectation for what athletes can accomplish. Furthermore, the expectation of physicality in sports carries an emphasis on bodies; it is common to inquire into which bodies are an advantage or a hindrance, what some are capable of, and how to track successful ones. This foregrounds analysis of observable traits of bodies, and therefore, socially constructed categories like race, gender, and ability—which Susan Birrell and Mary McDonald (2000) note must be understood in relation to each other.

The interplay between what individuals have been granted and what they are capable of earning yields sports tropes. Athletes in the Women's National Basketball Association (WNBA) play a classic form of basketball because they aren't capable of the modern style of the NBA. Black quarterbacks in the NFL can succeed by using their natural speed and strength rather than their developed passing skills or strategic thinking. Paralympic athletes are good within their own domain but aren't competing in "real" sport. These culturally hegemonic stereotypes, driven by the presumption of apolitical and meritocratic competition, gain the appearance of being natural. They appear not to be socially constructed and reinforced categories, merely truths exposed in the realm of competition. Sporting merit expresses and justifies social hierarchies while, as with sports in general, making them seem removed from their cultural context. Messages about ideology therefore seem real and appear to be justified through competition.

Assumptions about the pure competition of sports can also migrate from athletic contests into the business of sports management. Particularly with team sports organized into leagues, part of teams' success (or lack of it) can be attributed to management choices like personnel decisions, money allocation, and facilities. This association could seem like an outright incursion of the real world into the sphere of sports. However, since team management is held to have a direct link to competitive performance, it is also part of meritocracy. Better teams make better management decisions and therefore they are more likely to win. Supposedly each team has equal opportunity to make these decisions and some make better ones than others. Even explicit business decisions can fall under apolitical meritocracy. This is particularly important, since player management is regularly discussed in the business of sport. The descriptive and normative ways of viewing the players discussed earlier, therefore, come to be evaluated in economic ways. The supposed "real value" of players that unfolds through live competition gets assigned a dollar value. Their worth can then be the subject of analysis, discussion, and debate. Assigning monetary value based on perceived physical worth is a troubling practice rife in sports but normalized because it seems to be tracking actual value (Chapter 2).

The perception of pure competition constructs notions of not only individuals and institutions but also of temporality. The construction of the past becomes particularly powerful through the genre of live and real competition. Throughout the sports media and culture complex, sporting events of the past are told and retold. Slow motion and up-close replays during games, game recaps on sports news shows, biographies, documentaries, and fictional films, all support the notion that sports are live and real competition. They reproduce dominant narratives and myths, and—just as with the live experience of sports—their retelling obscures sports' ideologies by appearing to relay real events. For example, ESPN and Netflix's ten-part documentary series *The Last Dance* (2020) tells the story of Michael Jordan's last season with the NBA's Chicago Bulls. Though the series occasionally questions some of the myths generally associated with Jordan, it spends most of its time bolstering them. The series describes Jordan as not caring about anything besides winning, and subsequently earns his merit from mental and physical fortitude. In *The Last Dance*, the genre of documentary film merges with the genre of sport to communicate that the events transpired as told, and that the ideologies supported by those events are therefore vindicated. This holds for future sporting events as well; just as the real past is constructed, so too is the probable future. Narratives and prognostications shape expectations of events that have yet to happen and are structured by the same ideologies found throughout sports.

The ideologies of sports validated through the genre of live and real competition are received, interpreted, and engaged by fans. Like all fans, sports fans connect with their object of fandom in diverse ways and can even create non-hegemonic meanings. However, as with the generic expectations of sports, dominant meanings are found throughout the industry, texts, and fan engagement. Since hegemonic ideologies are confirmed and communicated through sports and sports media, they validate fans who already believe them. As noted earlier, the genre of sport increases their apparent validity, but the nature of sports fandom also renders hegemonic ideologies natural and self-evident. Though fandom generally involves identification with a fan object, this process is particularly powerful in sports fandom (Chapter 4). Identification is even found in the ways fans talk. It is common, for example, for fans to use the first-person plural *we* when discussing their team: "we won the championship" or "we should make a trade." This linguistic quirk isn't commonly found in other fandoms; though I am a fan of the *A Song of Ice and Fire* book series, I wouldn't say that "we"—meaning me and author George R. R. Martin—need to finish the sixth and seventh books. This deep fan identification allows fans to superimpose their values onto their object of fandom (Sandvoss, 2003). Given that sports seem live and real, the values read from the object of fandom seem to be justified. Rather than interpretations of a generic expectation, they instead seem real.

The genre of live and real competition has the tendency simultaneously to vindicate hegemonic ideology and make it seem apolitical, which makes it particularly worthy of critical intervention. Common ideological positions—like the GSM and the pureness of meritocracy—become channels for other ideologies about identity, bodies, government, and place. When one competitor triumphs over another, those ideologies infuse the victory with meaning without it seeming ideological. First, the competition creates hierarchies: winners and losers. Second, the competition's realness makes those hierarchies seem natural; they are grounded in some metaphysical or biological reality. Third, the fact that the real competition can be viewed live gives epistemic justification to the hierarchies; evidence for their reality plays out through the competition. The ideologies within and around sports, therefore, don't appear to be social constructions. They seem real and are apparently proven through the process of live competition. Again, this generic marker can be found in other contexts, but in sports and sports media we'll find it distilled down to a powerful and pronounced form. If the study of sports media is the study of the power of live and real competition, then its investigation will enable us to take lessons learned and apply them to other contexts.

Book Organization

The remainder of this book will advance my argument for the genre of live and real competition by demonstrating its presence throughout the sports and sports media complex. Indeed, it can be found in the structures that sell sport, create sports texts, and engage fans. Each chapter will survey a topic broad enough to demonstrate the reach of the genre throughout sports media but specific enough to go into detail. Each chapter will explore how research on these topics adds to and benefits from looking at sports as a genre.

Chapter 1 will focus on how sports media companies construct notions of liveness, realness, and competition for commodification. Newspapers; television channels; sponsors; websites; social media accounts; and even the sports leagues, teams, and athletes profit from the notion that sports are live and real competition. Chapter 2 will focus on the texts that the sports media industry produces. In particular, it will look at how representations of race, gender, class, ability, sexuality, and nationality gain credence through the generic expectation of live and real competition. In Chapter 3, we will consider the genre's relationship to live and real athlete expression, which is both a boon and a drawback for sports and sports media companies. We will analyze how the corporations shape how athletes communicate while still making it seem live and real—especially when it comes to activism against racism and for social justice. Chapter 4 will turn attention to fans of the sport genre. It will argue that expectation of live and real competition ties into how fans connect themselves to their object of fandom. The final chapter will focus on games built around sports, like fantasy sports, sports betting, and sports video games. We will see how these games depend upon sports' live and real competition.

By the end, I hope to have made the case for reframing of the study of sports media around live and real competition. This notion was always at work in the field, and this book simply takes the opportunity to illuminate and foreground it. In doing so, the field becomes clearly delineated despite not having a single methodology or theoretical affiliation. In fact, the diversity of approaches is a benefit, as the genre is expressed in many ways throughout the sports, media, and culture complex. Understanding sports media in this way draws connections between and paves inroads to researching sports media using interdisciplinary tools.

Bibliography

Andrews, D. & Giardina, M. (2008). Sport Without Guarantees: Toward a Cultural Studies That Matters. *Cultural Studies ↔ Critical Methodologies*, 8(4), 395–422.

Bernstein, A. & Blain, N. (2002). Sport and the Media: The Emergence of a Major Research Field. *Culture, Sport, Society*, 5(3), 1–30.

Billings, A. (2014). Reaction Time: Assessing the Record and Advancing a Future of Sports Media Scholarship. In A. Billings (Ed.), *Sports Media: Transformation, Integration, Consumption* (pp. 181–190). Routledge.

Birrell, S. & McDonald, M. (2000). Reading Sport, Articulating Power Lines: An Introduction. In S. Birrell & M. McDonald (Eds.), *Reading Sport: Critical Essays on Power and Representation* (pp. 3–13). Northeastern University Press.

Coakely, J. (2015). Assessing the Sociology of Sport: On Cultural Sensibilities and the Great Sport Myth. *International Review for the Sociology of Sport*, 50(4–5), 402–406.

Gantz, W. (2014). Keeping Score: Reflections and Suggestions for Scholarship in Sports and Media. In A. Billings (Ed.), *Sports Media: Transformation, Integration, Consumption* (pp. 7–18). Routledge.

Hargreaves, J. & McDonald, I. (2000). Cultural Studies and the Sociology of Sport. In J. Coakley & E. Dunning (Eds.), *Handbook of Sports Studies* (pp. 48–60). Sage.

Hill, A. (2015). *Reality TV*. Routledge.

Hutchins, B. & Rowe, D. (2012). *Sport Beyond Television: The Internet, Digital Media and the Rise of Networked Media Sport*. Routledge.

Jhally, S. (1989). Cultural Studies and the Sports/Media Complex. In L. Wenner (Ed.), *Media, Sports, & Society* (pp. 70–96). Sage.

Mittell, J. (2004). *Genre and Television: From Cop Shows to Cartoons in American Culture*. Routledge.

Mittell, J. (2017). Genre. In L. Ouellette & J. Gray (Eds.), *Keywords for Media Studies* (pp. 81–83). New York University Press.

Real, M. (2014). Theorizing the Sports-Television Dream Marriage: Why Sports Fit Television So Well. In A. Billings (Ed.), *Sports Media: Transformation, Integration, Consumption* (pp. 19–39). Routledge.

Rowe, D. (2004). *Sport, Culture and the Media*. Open University Press.

Sandvoss, C. (2003). *A Game of Two Halves: Football, Television and Globalization*. Routledge.

Seiter, E. (2006). Semiotics, Structuralism, and Television. In R. Allen (Ed.), *Channels of Discourse, Reassembled: Television and Contemporary Criticism* (pp. 31–66). University of North Carolina Press.

Serazio, M. (2019). *The Power of Sports: Media and Spectacle in American Culture*. New York University Press.

Suits, B. (1988). Tricky Triad: Games, Play, and Sport. *Journal of the Philosophy of Sport*, 9, 1–9.

Wenner, L. (1998). *MediaSport*. Routledge.

Whannel, G. (2000). Sport and the Media. In J. Coakley & E. Dunning (Eds.), *Handbook of Sports Studies* (pp. 291–308). Sage.

1
BRANDING LIVE AND REAL COMPETITION

While at dinner, a fan of the Los Angeles Lakers gets a notification from the ESPN app on her iPhone—a major trade has taken place. She quickly opens Twitter to read posts from NBA reporters employed by ESPN, Fox Sports, and the Atlantic. There's even a Photoshopped picture of the player in his new uniform sent from the Lakers' account, which was retweeted by the NBA. She walks over to the bar where, among the upscale liquor, televisions are tuned to ESPN. On the cable station, talking heads are analyzing what the trade means for the Lakers, the playoffs, and the NBA's power struggle between team owners and athletes. On the way back to her table, she sets a reminder on her phone to watch her favorite NBA YouTuber's most recent video about the trade on her computer. Amid the action, we can see the genre of live and real competition at play; a trade that has actual consequences for the Lakers' on-court success unfolds synchronously through multiple forms of media. In this chapter, we will consider how and why these kinds of experiences are constructed by sports media industries.

From the aforementioned anecdote, we can see why sports media are ubiquitous: engagements with sports are enabled by a network of different media and platforms. A feature of this diversity—like new media generally—is the tendency toward convergence (Hartley et al., 2013). Indeed, sports media exemplify both aspects of convergence. First, what were once separate engagements are currently enabled by a single technology. For example, text-based reporting, promotional images, and video analysis could all be found on the fan's phone. Second, separate functions that were enabled by a particular technology are now found across many different technologies (Jenkins, 2006). In other words, sports video commentary can be found across televisions, computers, and phones. If sports media are

DOI: 10.4324/9781003164272-2

distinguished by their generic markers, those markers must be found throughout these diverse opportunities to engage with them.

The sports genre coalesces on different platforms and media, and is constructed by a diverse set of creators. Different media producers—from huge companies with many outlets to an individual running a single vlog—participate in and make use of the expectations associated with live and real competition. Despite their dissimilarity, they all integrate the genre into their brands. Branding serves two crucial purposes for the sports genre. First, it helps manage and communicate genre-related expectations, values, and emotional connections (Lury, 2004; Banet-Weiser, 2012). Indeed, live and real sports are portrayed as exciting, fast-paced, and required viewing—themes that can be found throughout the sports media complex. Furthermore, the genre can help brands foster "authentic" affective connections (Banet-Weiser, 2012), as liveness and realness seem like the antithesis of being fabricated. Second, and related to the diverse and numerous entities that comprise the complex, brands structure the relationships between employers, employees, partners, and consumers (Lury, 2004). Structuring relationships, as we'll see later, allows large companies like the NBA and ESPN to manage many relationships. However, it is important to recognize that brands aren't created and maintained in a top–down fashion. Instead, the relationships connected by the brand collectively shape its meaning (Banet-Weiser, 2012; Arvidsson, 2006). While it is in the interests of a company to have a unified brand, it is constantly being constructed and reconstructed by a host of parties. These constituting relationships are found even among entities in the sports media industries that don't directly do business. In fact, the branded expectation of live and real competition is found even among rival corporations, since they all benefit from being connected to the genre. In this way, the entire complex of sports media industries supports generic values, expectations, feelings, and associations. To be part of the sports media industries is to promote liveness, realness, and competition.

In this chapter, we will survey how entities that comprise the industries of sports media integrate the sports genre into their brands. Since it would be impossible to give a comprehensive analysis of every aspect of the sports media industries, this chapter instead focuses on their most significant components. The first section will analyze how sports leagues and events construct the genre through competition on the field or court. The following section explores the genre's expression in sports journalism and broadcasting. To highlight what the sports genre can do for branding, its expression in other sites besides news and broadcasts—like sports documentaries and reality television—will be explored in the third section. By the end of this chapter, the pervasiveness and power of the branding work done by live and real competition throughout sports media industries will have been examined.

Sports Leagues and Events

While the genre is at work outside of competition, sports media revolve around epistemically uncertain contests that allow sports to be branded as live and real. That is, even though sports media are more than the mediation of live and real competition, the generic markers that originate in those competitions permeates the entire sports media complex. As the foundation for the genre, it is therefore important to begin with the games and the institutions that organize them. This section will consider how sports leagues and events construct, amplify, and protect the generic expectation. While a precise definition of "league" or "event" is difficult to capture, the focus of this section is placed on organizations like Major League Baseball (MLB), the NFL, and the Ultimate Fighting Championship (UFC), as well as events like National Collegiate Athletic Association (NCAA) football bowl games and the Olympic Games. Though the details of how each of these organizations are run and organized are incredibly different, they share common approaches to imbuing their brands with liveness and realness. Here we will focus on how leagues and events shape perception of their athletes and competition in order to make them consistent with generic expectations. These examples are also indicative of a much wider phenomenon.

Generally, the objectives of sports leagues and events are to "hire the best players, create contests with uncertain outcomes, and keep fans satisfied with the contests" (McFall, 2014, p. xii). Here we will consider the vital role of hiring and managing players in constructing the genre through protecting a sense of epistemic uncertainty. At first glance, the relationship between unpredictability and labor might not be obvious. But managing the athlete labor force is how leagues and events create contests that are competitive and, therefore, difficult to predict. In this section, we will explore how leagues and events manage their athlete labor force to augment epistemic uncertainty, thereby giving the feeling of live and real competition.

Feelings of uncertainty can arise even when players are highly managed, to the point that the details of the competition are largely scripted. Professional wrestling matches aren't pure competitions and are more like scripted events than most other sports. Beginning in the early 1900s, the results of wrestling competitions were fixed to avoid injuring the participants (Brown & Bryant, 2006, p. 90). While not every move in the ring is planned in advance, the important details of the match—like who wins or loses—are mostly predetermined (Hill, 2015, p. 107). However, knowledge of future results is tightly guarded to allow fans to experience the epistemic uncertainty that usually accompanies real competition. In this sense, professional wrestling is like fully scripted television shows—especially those known for surprising its audience like *Game of Thrones* or *Breaking Bad*—that try to capture the feeling of epistemic uncertainty that comes naturally with many sporting events. This epistemic connection to the sports genre justifies coverage of wrestling as though it were a sport, complete with news and highlight shows (Brown & Bryant, 2006, p. 91).

However, even leagues with truly unscripted competition foreground their liveness and realness. Specifically, organizing athlete acquisition and movement increase the sense of epistemic uncertainty that accompanies live and real competition. Mechanisms to do so are numerous, but some take the form of resource administration. Since professional leagues attract talent through salaries, leagues can attempt to distribute talent across its teams through resource management. For example, take revenue sharing, salary caps, and drafting talent. Revenue sharing tries to lessen the gap between the finances of the teams by redistributing resources from the highly profitable teams to those with less. Salary caps limit how much money teams can allocate to their players and therefore restrict the ability of well-off teams to outspend those that are less fortunate. Many leagues manage talent distribution from the players' entry into the leagues through a draft, in which teams select players according to a preassigned order. This order is often determined by previous competitive performance, with historically losing teams having the opportunity to pick earlier than teams with a winning record. By limiting the talent gaps between the top and bottom teams and moving them toward the mean, leagues can make its competitions more competitive.

The modes discussed earlier aren't the only ways to govern the athlete labor force for the ends of competitive parity. Consider the UFC, in which fighters are hired as independent contractors, burdening them with paying for their healthcare, training, and management (McClearen, 2021). A contractor system allows the UFC to control its fighters and inhibit unionization efforts (McClearen, 2021), but it also helps construct a system of epistemic uncertainty. The UFC determines who is fighting, when they fight, and where they fight. Therefore, it can schedule fights between fighters who are evenly matched or capable of creating hype. The wide varieties of fighting styles can also be tied to uncertainty; what happens when a top-tier wrestler takes on someone skilled at boxing? When tied to the precarity of employment, fighters are compelled to participate in the fight offered to them. Regardless of whether the fighter is healthy, fully prepared, or interested in the matchup, the UFC can leverage their power over their fighters in order to schedule fights that beg epistemic questions.

Live and real competition is also constructed through policies designed to "protect the integrity of the game." While leagues have always instantiated rules to make their games more regular or entertaining (Chandler, 1988), these rules were also put in place to protect the generic conventions of sports. Rules that regulate athletes' connections to gambling, PED use, and (for women's sports) supposed "gender misrepresentation" (a problematic concept to be critiqued later) are presented as safeguards of fairness. These rules set boundaries between what counts as part of the sport (and is therefore "fair") and outside of the sport (and is therefore "unfair"). If fans get the impression that outsiders like gamblers have predetermined the outcome of the game, then it becomes a loosely scripted performance rather than authentic competition. PEDs and "gender misrepresentation" are threats to real competition by giving the impression that one competitor or team is more likely to win due to considerations outside of the sport. However, what counts as "outside the sport," or even what to regulate, are largely determined by the leagues and events.

Athletes, for example, are allowed to enhance their performance with all sorts of substances. Sports leagues and events must decide which substances *appear* to harm the notion of real competition. Not every way of enhancing one's performance is prohibited, even if they involve drugs. Furthermore, playing games based on sports is extremely common, but leagues decide which kind of games are threats to the perception of live and real competition (in most cases, sports betting) and which aren't (commonly, season-long fantasy). Finally, Olympic gender testing is perhaps the most telling example of a sports institution creating a notion of fairness to protect the feeling of real competition. Gender tests are based on xenophobic, sexist, and racist ideologies, and gender has been historically defined based on arbitrary factors (Sloop, 2012). We will unpack the misogyny and transphobia inherent to these ideologies in the next chapter (along with their intersectional connections to race and nationality), but for now it is important to highlight that the International Olympic Committee (IOC) created policies to police the notion that men competing as women would be unfair. That's not to say that the IOC created sports-specific gender hierarchies and transphobia. Rather, its "gender verification" policies wrote them into the game by marking who gets to play ("insiders") and who gets treated with suspicion (potential "outsiders" who need to be eliminated). What counts as fair/unfair, real/unreal, and inside/outside is constructed by sports institutions. So it is ironic that scandals are often the result of their own policies.

Athletes who are caught and punished for supposedly illicit behavior damage the institutions' brands by raising questions about how often the behavior occurs throughout the sport. However, these behaviors are marked as illicit through the institutions' own policies. The policies meant to protect a notion of fair and real competition end up undermining that construction of fairness and realness when violations are found. This isn't to say that institutions aren't pressured to put certain policies in place. Instead, I argue that scandals reveal how some athlete behavior is marked as problematic based on how the sports institutions define what is a problem to real competition.

These violations can also be seen in polices intended to police athlete behavior during the competition. Since these rules pertain to what happens on the fields and courts, they attempt to shape what competition looks like. Some rules clearly regulate the competition itself—such as by prohibiting baseball pitchers having sticky substances on their hands—but many govern noncompetitive elements. Leagues like the NBA police how the players wear their uniforms, and the NFL has rules against taunting other players. We'll explore how sports organizations use policies like these to shape how their brand is represented in Chapter 2, but for the purposes of this chapter, it is important to see how they shape the competition on the field. These policies have nothing to do with protecting the game itself, and certainly don't aid in creating epistemic uncertainty—instead, they shape what the epistemically uncertain game looks like. These policies target Black athletes and are designed to shape their athletic performance to make the white commodity audience comfortable (Cunningham, 2009). Policies that shape the appearance of competition are rife with hegemonic ideologies. Because they regulate how the competition looks and is enforced, they end up becoming normalized as a part of live and real competition.

Live and real competition is also constructed by leagues when a potential scandal is downplayed. Consider the NFL's concealing of concussions and chronic traumatic encephalopathy (CTE). In 2013, the NFL settled a lawsuit with thousands of its retired players who alleged the league attempted to "conceal the link between football and brain damage" (Fainaru-Wada & Fainaru, 2013, p. 7). Though the NFL admitted no wrongdoing in its settlement, the players' case was a strong one, supported by the allegation that the NFL had put pressure on media outlets to downplay or ignore the CTE crisis (Oates, 2017, p. 165). Eventually, the attention was too much and the NFL established new rules and campaigns highlighting their concern for player safety (Oates, 2017, pp. 166–167). However, concussions and head trauma are still a part of the sport, with 281 reported in 2017, 214 in 2018, and 224 in 2019 (Battista, 2020; Reyes, 2020). The NFL still "packages hard-hitting action as imperative to [its] brand" (Siegel, 2019, p. 554).

Since concussions are associated with CTE, football still threatens player health. However, the institutional and game-based reasons for this danger are commonly ignored. For example, NBC's coverage of the NFL has discussed concussions mostly in terms of what the injury meant for the competition—like how an injury changed team strategy and whether "reckless" players who caused the injuries should be penalized (Mirer & Mederson, 2017). While it is clear why the NFL and its partners would react to the concussion controversy to protect their brand, for our purposes it is important to note that concussions remain an essential component of the NFL for reasons that are not being transparently explored. Concussions could be as discussed as other parts of the game, like strategies, player histories, and training regimens (Figure 1.1). Instead, the NFL obscures this very real aspect of the game. Unlike the aforementioned cases, head trauma is thought to be a natural part of the real competition and therefore, not scandalous. What qualifies as a component of live and real competition is constantly being managed by sports leagues and events.

The generic convention is created and sustained through rules and policies, especially those that shape and constrain athlete behavior. This is a stark incongruity; the leagues and events benefit from offering a product in which real competition plays out live, but the supposed real actions are constantly being

FIGURE 1.1 On *Fantasy Focus Football*, ESPN's injury expert Stephania Bell discusses whether the NFL's Evan Engram will play for the New York Giants due to concussion.

constrained by the organizations' interests. Though omnipresent and persistent, this tension is concealed because the generic construction of live and real competition is foregrounded over the organizations' role in constructing the genre. Dominant discourses about sports' purity of competition overwhelm the actions by leagues and events to shape their competitive events. Downplaying how organizations constrain players and events obscures the dominant ideologies that shape their policies and rules. Mandates that are racist, sexist, and xenophobic, for example, end up being presented as "just part of the game," and therefore become normalized.

Sports Journalism and Broadcasting

The sport–mass media relationship has been developing since the 1830s (McChesney, 1989, p. 49) and maybe even since colonial era (Bryant & Holt, 2006). The first known American sports story can be found in the *Boston Gazette* in 1733 (Enriquez, 2002, p. 198) and the first sports-specific magazine was created in the 1820s (Bryant & Holt, 2006). Sports journalism continued to develop in the latter half of the nineteenth century, during which sports-specific departments, sections, writers, and editors emerged (Mott, 1950). The coverage of sports grew along with other forms of entertainment like theater and vaudeville (Bellamy, 2006, p. 65). As an entertainment product, it had to distinguish itself among others. This section argues that news and media organizations echoed and constructed the genre of live and real competition as constructed by sports leagues. Leagues and news/media companies conspired to construct the markers of the genre. Indeed, sports coverage framed competition information in ways that marked sports as unique, interesting, and entertaining.

Print initially shaped the nature of sports and, by doing so, fashioned a more regular product. For example, *The American Turf Register and Sporting Magazine* (1829) and *Spirit of the Times* (1831) "did much to standardize thoroughbred racing across the nation by reporting exact weights and times and promulgating standards for betting and other rules" (Enriquez, 2002, p. 199). Standardization happened for boxing in the post-Civil War *Police Gazette* (Enriquez, 2002, p. 199). Early coverage of baseball "helped standardize and make more sophisticated the rules of and techniques for reporting about baseball, developing format innovations like box scores and detailed statistical analyses of pitching and hitting, which helped draw fans to the new league" (Bryant & Holt, 2006, p. 24). As leagues became more commodified and corporatized, newspapers responded by reporting on the economics of running a league or team (Boyle, 2006, p. 4). Coverage in early papers helped structure and organize sports and sports events.

For those unable to attend the game—and even for those who were in attendance trying to make sense of it afterwards—popular news sources presented the dominant account. However, the game was molded to draw readers' attention and shape the papers' commodity audience to be sold to advertisers. For example, Joseph Pulitzer, with his purchase of *New York World* in 1883, introduced illustrations to the sports stories to reach middle-class readers (Enriquez, 2002, p. 200). Charley Dryden, beginning in 1890, introduced engaging ways of writing about the game using slang and catchy nicknames (Enriquez, 2002, p. 200), and Grantland Rice later wrote eloquently about the drama of sports (Bryant & Holt, 2006, pp. 27–28). These early instantiations are a hallmark of sports writing: the presentation of sports in an engaging and approachable manner to garner interest.

An early innovator in sports writing was James Gordon Bennett, whose *New York Herald* used sensationalism to attract a wide audience appealing to advertisers (McChesney, 1989, p. 51; Enriquez, 2002, p. 199). Sensationalism could appeal to wider cultural and political conflicts; for instance, before the Civil War, newspapers covered major races between Northern and Southern horses (Enriquez, 2002, p. 198). In 1878, William B. Curtis, who became editor of the *Spirit of the Times*, used the notion of amateurism to privilege sports played by elites and degrade those played by working-class athletes (Enriquez, 2002, p. 199). In this way, the live and real competition was shaped by political and social debates to attract public fascination.

Sensationalism was one of the many techniques that led the journalistic integrity of sports reporting and reporters to be demeaned. Despite the appeals to sports' political and social importance, sports news tended to be viewed as less serious and lacking integrity. Sports news' negative perception partly stemmed from the relationship between sports leagues/teams and reporters. During the

1920s—the supposed Golden Age of Sports—writers were treated well by teams in order to get favorable publicity in their columns (Bryant & Holt, 2006, p. 28). These journalistic and ethical concerns "persist today, such that some newspapers refuse to allow their sports reporters to attend events without paying to enter the sports venue" and "[n]ewsroom colleagues also continue to be concerned about sports journalists who befriend athletes and thus do not keep professional distances from sources" (Wanta, 2006, p. 106). Due to the conflict of interest between coverage and access, sports reporting is often viewed as being uncritical (Sullivan, 2006, p. 142), contributing to the dumbing down of journalism (Boyle, 2006, p. 5) and lacking journalistic standards (Horky & Stelzner, 2015).

Sports remain a newspaper's "toy department," a negative perspective has been driven historically by what was covered and how it was covered. As an example of the former, as collegiate football grew in prominence, newspapers covered the social elite who attended the games rather than the games themselves (Enriquez, 2002, p. 200). Examples of the latter arise relatively often, even in contemporary sports media. One could write an entire book of controversies over ESPN's reporting and maybe even just of its relationship to the NFL. It was, for instance, perceived that ESPN broke ties with the *League of Denial* exposé on football and concussions due to pressure from the NFL (Vogan, 2015, pp. 171–174; Fainaru-Wada & Fainaru, 2013, pp. 353–355). More recently, ESPN NFL insider Adam Schefter was criticized when it was revealed in an email leak that he wrote to then-Washington Professional Football Team president Bruce Allen requesting to let him know if anything in his report "should be added, changed, tweaked" and ended with "Thanks, Mr. Editor, for that and the trust" (Jackson, 2021). Reported sporting events remain contentious.

Print, however, was a difficult way to capture the liveness and realness of sport. It's challenging to report on events that happen before, during, and after the competition, given the time needed to write, edit, print, and distribute the newspapers. Technological developments have offered different ways to engage with sports and thereby afforded novel ways to highlight live and real competition. The telegraph, for example, allowed sports information to be relayed quickly over large distances. It led to the establishment of pool rooms, which were spaces in which telegraphed sports details—horse races, in particular—were distributed to customers for betting purposes. These rooms helped capture the immediacy of live and real sports; a bettor need not wait until the publication of a race's results to find out whether their wagered money was won or lost. The telegraph took only minutes to capture and distribute the results. Furthermore, if the telegraph helped reinforce the notion of liveness, the newsreel did the same for realness. In the late nineteenth century, the newsreel became an opportunity for audiences to visualize sporting events they weren't present at (Bryant & Holt, 2006, p. 29). Both the newspaper and the telegraph-based pool room involved imaginative work on behalf of the sports fans; they must have read or listened to the account of the event and visualized what happened.

Radio in the 1920s was a draw as it allowed immediate access to sporting events and therefore brought the feeling of being present at a live sporting event. For this reason, radio was well suited for sports; after only a year of being on the market, radio was used to send sports information, meaning sports were a part of developing the new technology (Owens, 2006, p. 118). Outpaced by radio, newspapers turned to emphasizing new elements of the game, such as "in-depth discussions of strategy and analysis, personality profiles of great athletes, coaches, and executives, and coverage of off-the-field events" (Enriquez, 2002, p. 202). (Later, *Sports Illustrated* attempted similar maneuvers in response to the popularity of watching sports on television; the magazine offered engaging writing that explained *why* the events on television happened as they did. Groundbreaking photography (Enriquez, 2002, p. 204) alongside celebrity writers—like William Faulkner in 1955—helped the magazine gain credibility (Vogan, 2015, p. 81). This isn't to say, however, that the relationship between radio and print was always competitive. For example, in order to scoop the rivals *New York World* and *New York Journal* on coverage of the America's Cup yacht race, James Gordon Bennett Jr. paid a radio provider $5,000 to send information for quicker publication in his *New York Herald* (Owens, 2006, p. 118). Here we see the two media working in conjunction to sell the immediacy of live and real competition to prospective newspaper readers.

Radio broadcasts helped support sports that were becoming more organized and commodified in the 1920s and 1930s. However, those administering early baseball, boxing, and collegiate football occasionally had uneasy relationships with the popularizing technology. The friction often stemmed from who would be able to offer the live and real competition. The competition organizers used the draw of live sports to bring fans into the stadia and auditoriums. They worried that broadcasting radio accounts of the events would discourage attendance and therefore also suppress gate receipts. For this reason, all three professional New York baseball teams banned radio coverage in the 1930s (Gorman & Calhoun, 1994). Their concerns had historical precedent and anticipated future circumstances.

Racetrack and pool room operators were often at odds over the distribution of race information. Those who organized the track races viewed pool rooms as a threat (Sasuly, 1982, p. 75). This administrative tension resulted in a series of moves and countermoves. Pool room operators tried to smuggle out race information while track operators attempted to stop them. The most dramatic stories involved shooting down information-carrying balloons and sealing shut bathroom windows used to pass race details. Both the telegraph- and radio-based struggles over game information anticipated the television industry practice of blacking out the broadcasts of games in local markets. These conflicts over who gets to profit from the live competition shows that, even early on, there was value placed on the liveness of sports. It is still assumed that media technology can capture the liveness of sports to the point that people won't feel the need to pay to watch the event in person.

Game broadcasts weren't the only sports content available on radio; sports news and talk shows have also historically been popular. The latter have given rise to many celebrity commentators, including contemporary examples like Jim Rome, Colin Cowherd, Mike Greenberg, Mike Golic, Chris Russo, Mike Francesa, and Dan Le Batard. They all brought their own personalities and opinions into the discussion of the daily sports stories. Relying on the liveness of radio, these commentators could respond in the moment to the events of the day. Radio talk shows, therefore, offered the opportunity to see both how live and real sports were constructed by the "takes" of the commentators and benefited from the constant flow of live and real sports stories. When, for example, research demonstrates how Jim Rome's nationally syndicated radio show reinforced hegemonic masculinity (Tremblay & Tremblay, 2001; Nylund, 2004), it is important to note that those meanings also shaped the genre of sport. While we'll consider representation more closely in Chapter 2, personality-driven radio shows like Rome's infused live and real sport with ideologies about gender and sexuality (Tremblay & Tremblay, 2001; Nylund, 2004).

If radio captured the liveness of sports in novel ways that previous media didn't, television built on previous media. Like radio, it offered the feeling of immediacy, and like newsreels, it allowed audiences to see the events and therefore added to a sense of realness. The light, movement, sound, and "liveness" of the medium gave television—and therefore sports on television—"a reality of its own" (Real, 2014, p. 21). As televised sports matured, so did their appeal to the liveness and realness of sports. Eventually, live sporting events became a form of prestige content for sports media companies to gain credibility and stand out from their competitors (Mondello, 2006, p. 278). Leagues with major broadcasting rights deals now shape their entertainment product toward being televised (Fortunato, 2015). The genre of sports, as expressed through television, was simultaneously built by sports leagues and broadcasters. For this reason, television broadcasters innovated to highlight the novelty of the sports genre.

Roone Arledge, an influential producer and eventual president for ABC Sports, held that watching a game on TV should be like being there in person. His network's broadcasts captured what happened on the field, as well as in the stands and sidelines (Bryant & Holt, 2006, p. 34). Using more cameras than previous broadcasts and on-field microphones, he manufactured the feeling of in-stadia sports. Arledge, therefore, constructed not just the competition but also what it was like to *be at* the competition. His desire to manufacture a feeling of "being there" echoes throughout sports broadcasts' use of more contemporary technologies. The development of high-definition television, for example, allowed for what seemed like "a more realistic viewing experience" than previous broadcast formats (Brown & Bryant, 2006, p. 101). Tickers displaying scores and news at the bottom of the television screen brought a feeling that the sports world was always developing with the speed of the stock market. Along with using the cameras' focus to structure the event, Arledge also used instant replay and graphics to aid in the process (Bryan & Holt, 2006, p. 34). His mics picked up sound unheard by fans in the stadia, and those watching at home saw the game from multiple angles and occasionally in slow motion rather than from one perspective. Game commentary was available only to those listening to the broadcasters. Arledge's advancements created a mediated construction of being present at the game—not merely a reflection of it.

As with radio, the narration and commentary of a televised broadcast plays a role in organizing the images and sounds supplied. The commentary "mediate[s] the viewer's experience of the sports event" (Sullivan, 2006, p. 139), and therefore is an opportunity for broadcasters to shape the live and real competition. Arledge, for example, encouraged commentators to "dramatize and personalize the event" (Bryan & Holt, 2006, p. 34). One consistent frame used throughout televisual sports broadcasts to create drama is conflict: "broadcast TV uses camera coverage and commentary as tools to identify, focus on, and interpret key moments of conflict" (Sullivan, 2006, p. 138). Conflict is infused with emotion and aggression (Sullivan, 2006) and amplifies sports' melodrama (Johnson, 2021, p. 118). There are, certainly, other frames that could be foregrounded—such as the increase in statistics and prediction due to the fantasy sports boom of the early 2000s (Wood & Benigni, 2006, p. 166)—but it is vital to the games' success that they were manufactured to put conflict first.

Conflict is dramatized further when it plays out live and seems real. The innovations pioneered by Arledge helped live television broadcasts construct the feeling of an in-stadia, live viewing of sports. It is important to highlight, however, that this remains only a feeling—a constructed liveness. What is represented as being "live and at the game" can be distinguished from what it is actually like to be in the stadium or on the sidelines. Indeed, the visual devices described earlier "may grab viewer attention at the expense of realism" (Sullivan, 2006, p. 138). The history of televised sports is littered with innovations that fans were initially skeptical of or even rejected, like the "glow puck" of Fox's coverage of the National Hockey League (NHL) (Johnson, 2021, pp. 69–73). Amid the entire spectacle, the game itself might recede into the background (Sandvoss, 2003). In this way, what is considered "liveness" and "realness" becomes removed from the actual game and is constructed by generic markers used and reused throughout televisual broadcasts and sports media.

Leagues reacted to the success of broadcast sports by enacting rule changes, like the two-minute warning in football, stroke play in golf, shot clock in basketball (Sullivan, 2006, p. 137), and TV-friendly scheduling (Rader, 1984). There was even a short-lived period in which home field advantage for MLB's World Series was determined by the results of the All-Star game. This was partially the result of pressure from the rights holder of the All-Star Game (Fox) to make the game matter to fans more (Wood & Benigni, 2006, p. 157). MLB's All-Star Game can be categorized as a "pseudoevent" like the Super Bowl—events that are the co-creation of the media and sports leagues (Boorstin, 1964). The Super Bowl, for example, was "conceived as a media event in 1976 [and] would not have occurred if not for the promise of network TV exposure" (Sullivan, 2006, p. 134). Media like television don't just capture the liveness and realness of sports; they shape the competition itself.

Live and real competition is formed by more than the drive to build an entertaining media product; it is also a promotional vehicle. Advertisements can now be found throughout stadia, on uniforms, and in announcers' commentary (Figure 1.2). Corporations choose their sponsorships based on perceived fit with the sport (Kinney, 2006, p. 299), which is tied to live and real competition. Furthermore, given the fans' desire to watch live events, the commercials cannot be fast-forwarded as when watching a recorded game. In this way, broadcasters benefit from the notion that sports, and especially sports mega events, are "zap-proof." In other words, "it is impossible for the viewer to avoid advertising messages without missing part of the sports event" (Bellamy, 2006, p. 72). While it can be argued that all broadcasts are centered on "the circulation of commodities" (Jhally, 1989, p. 79), the

FIGURE 1.2 A broadcast of a match between the National Women's Soccer League (NWSL)'s Portland Thorns and San Diego Wave which includes ads for Ally Financial, Umpqua Bank, Dutch Bros Coffee, Delta Airlines, Mastercard, and NWSLsoccer.com.

Super Bowl is a live event that shows how the commercials are as much a part of the spectacle as the game itself (Brown & Bryant, 2006, p. 83). The live and real competition simultaneously benefits media companies, leagues, and sponsors and is shaped by these advertisements. It becomes impossible to separate the live and real game from its consumerist ideologies.

Exclusivity powerfully affects how radio and television broadcasts shape the sports genre. Partnerships in which sports leagues sell exclusive content to broadcasters grant them considerable control over shaping an event. There is certainly a diverse set of ways any individual sporting event can be captured and distributed that involves many different corporations and forms of media; for instance, a Super Bowl game could be covered by live tweets from a journalist, captured for a documentary or online content by the NFL, and used in a Nike ad after it ends. However, the NFL's broadcast deals with ABC, NBC, CBS, and Fox allow those companies to be a primary way consumers engage with the live events. Those attracted to the unique affordances of a television broadcast, due to exclusive rights, are compelled to have the event shaped by the broadcasting company. These exclusive games are a "perishable product" that creates a "demand for up-to-the-moment match and event results by fans" (Hutchins & Rowe, 2012, p. 21). While fans might get current information from online sources like social media, the broadcast is a primary source for watching the game. The perishability of synchronously engaging with sports also lends itself to sports' supposed "zap-proof" nature. The value of exclusivity and perishability are intimately tied to the generic convention of liveness; sport uniquely happens live and perishes when the moment is over.

The value of having exclusive access to a perishable live and real product also is revealed when it is sold directly to sports fans. Before in-home television's popularization, closed-circuit television was broadcasted to audiences at a price (Johnson, 2021, p. 146). Fans would gather in groups to watch the broadcasts, and it quickly became clear that sports—particularly boxing—was most popular (Johnson, 2021, p. 149). For example, the 1951 bout between Joe Louis and Lee Savold in Madison Square Garden drew 18,179 fans, with over 39,000 additional fans watching in closed-circuit television (Vogan, 2018, p. 3). These public broadcasts combined elements of liveness and realness found on television with the feeling of cheering alongside fellow fans in the stadium. Closed-circuit television proved the value of the feeling of liveness and realness, even if it was manufactured through a broadcast and happening outside of the stadia. Even pay-per-view—the ancestor of closed-circuit television in which the event can be viewed at home for a price—shows the value of being at a live competition.

The worth of being the exclusive site for engagement emerged at the beginning of sport's commodification. When it was realized that people would pay to watch sports, certain barriers were erected to deny access to those who didn't pay for attendance. The high cost of attending sports events can attest to the value of seeing the real competition live. Broadcast rights were the mediated version of stadia and arenas; only those who paid (as in pay-per-view or cable) or who were paid for (as in commercial broadcast television) received access to watch the event. Wherever people are willing to pay—at a stadium, at a bar, or at home—the genre of sports, delivered live, has always been a significant draw.

Sports journalism and broadcasting reinforced and shaped the feeling that sports was a unique entertainment genre. While other genres might have elements of realness, liveness, and/or competition, the blend of the three constructed in the coverage of sporting events created value and sustained interest. Since they involved competition, there was a sense of drama that could be constructed and highlighted. Since that competition played out in front of an audience, attempts to capture and construct the liveness of the drama through media were warranted. Since the live drama was unscripted, it warranted news-like coverage like other real-world events. Again, like all genres, the boundaries between the genre of sports and others are permeable; competition reality television shows like *Top Chef* and *RuPaul's Drag Race*, for instance, can share similar generic constructions. However, through sports journalism and broadcasts we see the pervasiveness of these constructions partially through their long-standing histories.

Sports Media's Diversity

Televisual broadcasts have been thought to be particularly well suited for sports since they captured the liveness associated with the competitions. However, such medium-specific acclaim is coming into the question with the development of newer media outlets and technologies (Rowe, 2014, p. 94), extending a pattern we saw earlier; the telegraph afforded ways of capturing live and real competition that differed from print and radio. This section will highlight the diversity of other platforms that sports outlets can use to reference live and real competition.

It is perhaps most helpful to start with ESPN, given its prevalence and power in the realm of sports. ESPN started as the Entertainment and Sports Programming Network (ESP Network, for short) in 1979, as the first channel dedicated exclusively to sports (Wood & Benigni, 2006, p. 149). ESPN strove to distinguish itself as *the* place for sports coverage and to equate itself with sports fandom (Vogan, 2015, p. 34). Part of its strategy involved offering live broadcasts of sporting events that weren't covered elsewhere, like the early rounds of the NCAA basketball tournament, MLB's hall of fame induction ceremony, and the NFL draft (Vogan, 2015, pp. 23–24). Furthermore, ESPN used *SportsCenter* as a flagship show that centered its lifestyle brand (Vogan, 2015, pp. 31, 34).

As a news and highlight show, *SportsCenter* recapped sporting events with flair novel to ESPN; popular anchors like Dan Patrick and Keith Olbermann quipped their way through the day's games with notable catchphrases (Enriquez, 2002, p. 206). Due to being broadcast live in many cases (Brown & Bryant, 2006, p. 82), the anchors' witticisms seemed like clever, improvised, and in-the-moment reactions to the unscripted sports action. Therefore, ESPN's lifestyle brand, as expressed through *SportsCenter*, was formed through the expectation that sports engagement was live and real—even when recapping the events of the day. The popularity of the show's highlights led some to pontificate about their effects on the sports themselves. They speculated that athletes perhaps had changed their play to be more worthy of being broadcast on *SportsCenter* (Brown & Bryant, 2006, p. 100; Wood & Benigni, 2006, pp. 156–157); the look of the live and real competition would be influenced by the players' decisions to play in a highlight-worthy fashion. If true, this would demonstrate that even the aesthetics of the live and real game are constructed.

As ESPN grew, it added multiple other channels that each highlighted and adapted different aspects of the sports genre. In its inception, for example, ESPN2 targeted "young and light to moderate sports viewers" (Wood & Benigni, 2006, p. 147), by branding itself in ways akin to MTV (Vogan, 2015, p. 36). Its format involved mixing sports highlights with music, airing less formal and structured shows and commentators, and hiring MTV hosts like "Downtown" Julie Brown as well as shock jocks, like the aforementioned Jim Rome (Vogan, 2015, p. 36). Other ESPN channels demonstrated the multitude of ways that live and real competition could be formulated. ESPN News focused on sports news, ESPN Classic on constructing sports history, and ESPN U on collegiate sports. Each channel had its own way of framing sports; sports as news differed from the usual narratives about amateurism and playing for the love of the game that surrounded collegiate sports. In this way, ESPN drew on liveness and realness to create a multifaceted brand across many different channels.

Of course, ESPN's connection to the genre of sports was also expressed in its role in the larger Disney conglomerate. With Disney's acquisition of ESPN in 1996, ESPN transformed "into a synergy-driven and multiplatform corporate subconglomerate" (Vogan, 2015, p. 3). Disney moved its sports content under the ESPN umbrella in 2006, rebranding ABC Sports to *ESPN on ABC* and moved *Monday Night Football* to ESPN (Vogan, 2015, p. 39). ESPN, therefore, became the space for live and real competition in Disney just as *Star Wars* became the place for science fiction, Marvel for superheroes, and Pixar for children's movies.

Perhaps the most transparent way to see media's construction of the genre is through documentary film and reality television shows. A diverse set of organizations now produces sports documentaries, including HBO, ESPN, the NFL, and PBS. Though sports documentaries have been around since the 1960s, they boomed in the 1990s (Vogan, 2015, p. 46). Since documentaries are viewed with esteem, entities like HBO can integrate sports documentaries into their prestige programming, while PBS aligns them with their civic-minded values (Vogan, 2015, p. 44). Sports docs, therefore, allow media companies to draw on the genre of live and real competition that's usually lacking into their brands. This goes the other way, too. Sports media companies can also fold documentaries into their brands. Take, for instance, ESPN's use of *SportsCentury* to compete against sports documentary frontrunners HBO and PBS (Vogan, 2015, p. 47). The genre of sports becomes prestige entertainment when connected to HBO or the documentary film genre.

ESPN's *SportsCentury* stands as a potent example of how the specific generic conventions of sport and documentary support each other. Travis Vogan (2015) examines how the docuseries accorded with and shaped ESPN's broader brand. Premiering in 1998, *SportsCentury* was "an eighteen-month trans-media event that reflected on the twentieth century's greatest North American sports figures and moments" (Vogan, 2015, p. 43). The cornerstone of the event was a ranking of the century's top 100 athletes and corresponding documentary profiles of the top 50 (Vogan, 2015, p. 44). *SportsCentury* producers used documentary generic conventions to legitimize its historical account; interviews laid out to "fashion . . . a sober, scholarly historical register" (Vogan, 2015, p. 48), "a prominent group of expert panelists and interviewees" for credibility's sake, (Vogan, 2015, p. 48), and historical footage all set the expectation that the documentaries captured things as they really occurred. Of course, the series was intended to cause debate and successive engagement with ESPN properties (Vogan, 2015, p. 49) and not to question that the events occurred as described.

When the power of the generic expectations of sports combined with the generic conventions of documentary film, the resulting assumption was that *SportsCentury* faithfully captured sports history. Furthermore, because the series was produced by a company synonymous with sports, that feeling became only more entrenched. This is extremely concerning, as many researchers have raised problems with the show's representation of gender; it included only seven women, a race horse (Secretariat) outranked four of those women, and it often relied on worrisome stereotypes (Billings, 2000; Spencer, 2003). In Chapter 2, we'll further discuss the problems with expressing harmful stereotypes and ideologies through the genre of sports. For this chapter's purpose, it is important to recognize the interplay of the generic conventions in sports documentaries, particularly how they combine to enforce the feeling of live and real competition.

The conventions and expectations of both genres also complement each other in sports reality television. Even though reality TV isn't considered to be prestige like documentary film, they share an expectation that what is being represented has a connection to reality. While viewers are aware that the shows have been produced and edited, they still hold the belief that the events depicted occurred in some fashion. Reality competition shows are a particularly good fit for the genre of live and real competition, as they represent the opportunity to infuse the behind-the-scenes drama of reality TV with the competitive element of sports. *The Contender* and *Knight School* represent early attempts by ESPN to get into the reality game by following boxing hopefuls and walk-on collegiate basketballers, respectively (Vogan, 2015, p. 99). ESPN remains in this space today with UFC's *The Ultimate Fighter*. Viewers get to see a unified construction of narratives, inside and outside the octagon, which encourage and reify the feeling of reality. Even shows that don't involve competition still lend credence to sports' generic convention of reality. Athlete and coach profiles, for instance, give the sense that they are capturing the actual personalities and stories of those involved in sports. They convey the impression that fans get to see the athletes and coaches as they really are, both during and away from the competition. For this reason, NBC tries to mix their coverage of the Olympics with athlete profiles; people get more emotionally invested when they feel as though they know who is competing and are connected to their narratives. ESPN is committed to this format, and athlete profiles—*The Boardroom, Alex Morgan: The Equalizer, Why We Fight, Claressa Shields, Peyton's Places, More Than an Athlete*—are found throughout their ESPN+ online subscription service.

Hard Knocks is a helpful example of how sports, documentary, and reality TV genres can support and reinforce each other's generic expectations. It is a show that "purports to offer unprecedented access into the daily operations of NFL training camps, following players, coaches, and management during practices, workouts, meetings, and ever after hours" (Vogan, 2011, p. 293). Behind-the-scenes access captures features of the NFL that are unseen by most. For example, in the show audiences get to see how coaches run practice and engage with players (Vogan, 2014, p. 66), how athletes behave during practice, and even when players get cut from the team (Vogan, 2014, p. 158). When combined with the interpersonal drama of reality TV and documentary film conventions like "voice-of-god narration, on-field sound, montage editing, and original scores" (Vogan, 2014, p. 158), the show brands itself as being accurate representations. *Hard Knocks* purports to capture the reality of the NFL.

It is worth considering how the reality of sports can even be inherited by fictional and fictionalized sports movies. While the drama in sports docudramas like *Brian's Song* and *Pride of the Yankees* comes from the understanding that something like the events depicted actually occurred—a feeling that could be strengthened by the use of actual game footage during the movie (Vogan, 2015, p. 106)—all sports movies appeal to the wider expectation that sports are real and can be watched live. The thrill of heroic victories and underdog stories draw from the idea that these sports stories happened. Even futuristic fictional sports like those depicted in *Rollerball, Star Wars: The Phantom Menace, The Hunger Games* series, and *Alita: Battle Angel* build on the appeal of live and real competition.

Finally, the genre of sports is now also formed online. Being constituted online is important, because "when people talk of the screen that delivers them footage of their favorite professional sport, many are talking about desktop, laptop, and tablet computer screens as well as television" (Hutchins & Rowe, 2012, p. 4). While Chapter 4 will consider how fans use the Internet, this chapter will focus on its use by journalistic and media entities, tracking how the affordances of the Internet allow for a novel expression of some of the mechanisms by which the genre of sports is constructed that were surveyed earlier. For example, many of the concerns about sports journalism have escalated for online sports news. Critics have argued that online sports commentary and analysis are unprofessional, lack oversight, and biased (Vogan, 2015, p. 79). For this reason, companies interested in having an online presence seek to establish credibility. For example, in its development of *Page 2*, ESPN recruited known writers like David Halberstam, Hunter S. Thompson, and Ralph Wiley who were known for "probing sport's cultural resonances" (Vogan, 2015, p. 81). ESPN hoped their online accounts of and thoughts on sports would be respected, unlike the usual perception of Internet journalism. This strategy was later also used in 2011 by ESPN and Bill Simmons to brand *Grantland*. Named after the aforementioned Grantland Rice, the site highlighted celebrity editors and contributors—David Cho, Lane Brown, Dan Fierman, Rafe Bartholomew, Dave Eggers, Malcolm Gladwell, Chuck Klosterman, Jane Leavy, Chris Jones, Katie Baker, and Tom Bissell—to create an *Esquire*- or *GQ*-like brand for more sophisticated, long-form online sports commentary (Vogan, 2015, pp. 148–149). Simmons applied this strategy yet again in 2016 for his own sports and popular culture media company, *The Ringer*. ESPN also continues to use personalities to brand how its websites engage with the genre of sport; for example, Nate Silver's *FiveThirtyEight* tackles sports (along with popular culture and politics) from a statistical perspective.

Streaming of games is becoming commonplace online. In fact, it is currently difficult to find a game being broadcast on television that isn't also streamable. A Monday Night Football NFL game on ESPN is found also on its website and mobile application. Furthermore, companies use exclusively broadcasting games online as ways to drive subscriptions for their online platforms. ESPN attracts viewers to its online destinations through the UFC, Bundesliga Soccer, and the NBA G League (Lopez, 2022). NBC does the same for its Peacock app with the English Premier League, and CBS for Paramount+ using UEFA's Champions League and the National Women's Soccer League. These broadcasts, despite increasing the diversity of modes of engagement with the competitions, "are still largely enhancements of the 'ultimate' live sports viewing experience, or compensation for an inability to simulate plausibly, in smaller or larger scale . . . the embodied collective experience of the crowd" (Rowe, 2014, p. 99).

It is worth focusing on ESPN+ because it demonstrates the breadth of offerings that a sports subscription service can offer. ESPN+ provides engagements with sports well beyond the broadcasting of games and therefore has created opportunities to shape and be shaped by the genre of live and real competition. For example, ESPN+ offers the *30 for 30* documentary film collection, reality TV series, and athlete profiles. The subscription fee also includes resources for sports gaming: March Madness bracket predictors, advice on fantasy sports, and sports betting information. We'll see in Chapter 5 how games like these support the genre of sports, but here it is enough to note that ESPN+ draws on the unpredictability of sports as a mechanism in these prediction games. Sports gaming directly uses the expectations that sports are live and competition is real to drive attention to games.

ESPN+ is also just one component of ESPN's wider online presence. In fact, it is represented on ESPN's main website and mobile application as a subscription-based add-on to its sports coverage, broadcasts, and gaming opportunities. Whether the content is free or comes with a cable or ESPN+ subscription, it demonstrates sports' digital convergence. In this way, ESPN's attempt to construct itself as synonymous with sports has been aided by the merging of online affordances and the genre of sport. As we've seen, ESPN's online products unite sports-specific coverage, broadcasting, and gaming. Immediate information about one's favorite team, a broadcast of a matchup of one's favorite league, and strategy about one's favorite sports-based game all converge in one place.

The genre of sports is also expressed online through platforms not owned and run by sports media companies. Indeed, all sports companies have a robust presence on social media platforms they don't own like Facebook, Twitter, and Instagram. Rather than exploring how fans engage with the genre on social media (Chapter 4), here we will consider how media companies like ESPN use the particular affordances of social media in order to express the generic conventions of live and real competition. Social media are a particularly good fit for the genre. Just as radio brought the ability to disseminate sports information more quickly than print, thus heightening the sensation of liveness, social media affords unique opportunities to develop aspects of the genre that were underdeveloped in previous media. That is, they express aspects of the genre we've seen previously in new ways. Take, for instance, the conflict over information. News and media companies strive to be the first and most accurate source of sports news, while sports leagues and teams attempt to control the information released by media and how they present it (Boyle, 2006, p. 132). Social media offer a way to circumvent this struggle and allow leagues and teams to be the first to share their manicured version of the story (Price et al., 2013). It is certainly the case that team- and league-owned websites allow a similar release of information, but fans may not check them. Social media posts are ways to reach out to fans by popping up in their feeds. The drive for immediate information about live and real events that was commodified by news and media companies can be, with the help of social media, usurped by sports teams and leagues.

Conclusion

It should be recognized that the line drawn between sports organizations and sports media in this chapter, while conceptually helpful, is artificial. Sports leagues and teams have always produced their own media, and media companies have always sought ownership in sports. This is especially true in the contemporary sports/media complex. Teams and leagues create and disseminate their own media through cable broadcasts, mobile applications, and social media. For their part, media companies invest in sports events, teams, and leagues. This means that, while the construction of the sports genre happens across a diverse and disaggregated sports/media complex, it often is the result of a single corporation's control over a diverse set of assets. ESPN, for example, can put on the *X Games*, broadcast them across its channels, and cover them online, all the while using its control over the entire network to infuse it with its brand's values. Part of this process relies on the belief that the *X Games* are live and real competition that warrants media coverage.

Therefore, this way of conceiving of sport and media as separate entities is merely an organizational heuristic used for this chapter. Indeed, it is valuable to conceptualize sport as media (Hutchins & Rowe, 2012, p. 10). It follows that the generic conventions aren't constructed by media *or* sports organizations; instead, they are formed by the unity of the two. The entities mentioned earlier—consisting of sports leagues, teams, news organizations, sports magazines, radio and TV broadcasts, documentary films, reality television, Internet commentary, and advertisers (among others)—all form a multimedia complex that construct and benefit from the expectation that sports are live and real competition.

This sports/media complex is incredibly diverse and is a mixture of sports leagues and organizations, players, media companies, journalistic entities, and corporate sponsors and partners. And yet, despite this diversity, they all construct the genre of live and real competition. Even corporations that are competitors share from being connected to the values and associations of the genre. Different companies might shape the conventions to their brand differently—Fox and ESPN, for instance, might fold the genre into their divergent brands distinctly—but being connected to sports comes with certain overall expectations that are profitable. For this reason, across the sports/media complex, the genre of sports is fairly stable, despite all of the diversity of the sports media universe.

Bibliography

Arvidsson, A. (2006). *Brands: Meaning and Value in Media Culture*. Routledge.
Banet-Weiser, S. (2012). *Authentic™: The Politics of Ambivalence in a Brand Culture*. New York University Press.
Battista, J. (2020). NFL Reveals 2019 Injury Data, Hopeful Rule Changes Are Working. *NFL.com*. www.nfl.com/news/nfl-reveals-2019-injury-data-hopeful-rule-changes-are-working-0ap3000001098679
Bellamy, R. (2006). Sports Media: A Modern Institution. In A. Raney & J. Bryant (Eds.), *Handbook of Sports and Media* (pp. 63–76). Routledge.
Billings, A. (2000). In Search of Women Athletes: ESPN's List of the Top 100 Athletes of the Century. *Journal of Sport and Social Issues*, 24(4), 415–421.

Boorstin, D. (1964). *The Image: A Guide to Pseudo-Events in America*. Vintage Books.
Boyle, R. (2006). *Sports Journalism: Context and Issues*. Sage.
Brown, D. & Bryant, J. (2006). Sports Content on U.S. Television. In A. Raney & J. Bryant (Eds.), *Handbook of Sports and Media* (pp. 77–104). Routledge.
Bryant, J. & Holt, A. (2006). A Historical Overview of Sports and Media in the United States. In A. Raney & J. Bryant (Eds.), *Handbook of Sports and Media* (pp. 21–44). Routledge.
Chandler, J. (1988). *Television and National Sport: The United States and Britain*. University of Illinois Press.
Cunningham, P. (2009). "Please Don't Fine Me Again!!!!!": Black Athletic Defiance in the NBA and NFL. *Journal of Sport and Social Issues*, 33(1), 39–58.
Enriquez, J. (2002). Coverage of Sports. In W. Sloan & L. Mullikin Parcell (Eds.), *American Journalism: History, Principles, Practices* (pp. 198–208). McFarland & Company.
Fainaru-Wada, M. & Fainaru, S. (2013). *League of Denial: The NFL, Concussions, and the Battle for Truth*. Three Rivers Press.
Fortunato, J. (2015). Television Broadcast Rights: Still the Golden Goose. In P. Peterson (Ed.), *Routledge Handbook of Sport Communication* (pp. 188–196). Routledge.
Gorman, J. & Calhoun, K. (1994). *The Name of the Game: The Business of Sports*. Wiley.
Hartley, J., Burgess, J. & Bruns, A. (2013). *A Companion to New Media Dynamics*. John Wiley & Sons.
Hill, A. (2015). *Reality TV*. Routledge.
Horky, T. & Stelzner, B. (2015). Sports Reporting and Journalistic Principles. In P. Peterson (Ed.), *Routledge Handbook of Sport Communication* (pp. 118–127). Routledge.
Hutchins, B. & Rowe, D. (2012). *Sport Beyond Television: The Internet, Digital Media and the Rise of Networked Media Sport*. Routledge.
Jackson, W. (2021). Adam Schefter Addresses Email Scandal: "It Was a Step too Far." *SI.com*. www.si.com/nfl/2021/10/14/adam-schefter-addresses-bruce-allen-email-washington-football-team-investigation
Jenkins, H. (2006). *Convergence Culture: Where Old and New Media Collide*. New York University Press.
Jhally, S. (1989). Cultural Studies and the Sports/Media Complex. In L. Wenner (Ed.), *Media, Sports, & Society* (pp. 70–96). Sage.
Johnson, V. (2021). *Sports TV*. Routledge.
Kinney, L. (2006). Sports Sponsorship. In A. Raney & J. Bryant (Eds.), *Handbook of Sports and Media* (pp. 295–310). Routledge.
Lopez, J. (2022). ESPN+: Subscribing to Diversity, Marginalizing Women's Sports. In D. Johnson (Ed.), *From Networks to Netflix: A Guide to Changing Channels* (2nd ed.). (pp. 337–385). Routledge.
Lury, C. (2004). *Brands: The Logos of the Global Economy*. Routledge.
McChesney, R. (1989). Media Made Sport: A History of Sports Coverage in the United States. In L. Wenner (Ed.), *Media, Sports, & Society* (pp. 49–69). Sage.
McClearen, J. (2021). *Fighting Visibility: Sports Media and Female Athletes in the UFC*. University of Illinois Press.
McFall, T. (2014). *The (Peculiar) Economics of NCAA Basketball*. Palgrave MacMillan.
Mirer, M. & Mederson, M. (2017). Leading with the Head: How NBC's Football Night in America Framed Football's Concussion Crisis, a Case Study. *Journal of Sports Media*, 12(1), 21–44.

Mondello, M. (2006). Sports Economics and the Media. In A. Raney & J. Bryant (Eds.), *Handbook of Sports and Media* (pp. 277–294). Routledge.

Mott, F. (1950). *American Journalism: A History of Newspapers in the United States through 260 Years: 1960 to 1950.* MacMillan.

Nylund, D. (2004). When in Rome: Heterosexism, Homophobia, and Sports Talk Radio. *Journal of Sport & Social Issues*, 28(2), 136–168.

Oates, T. (2017). *Football and Manliness: An Unauthorized Account of the NFL.* University of Illinois Press.

Owens, J. (2006). The Coverage of Sports on Radio. In A. Raney & J. Bryant (Eds.), *Handbook of Sports and Media* (pp. 117–130). Routledge.

Price, J., Farrington, N. & Hall, L. (2013). Changing the Game? The Impact of Twitter on Relationships between Football Clubs, Supporters and the Sports Media. *Soccer & Society*, 14(4), 446–461.

Rader, B. (1984). *In Its Own Image: How Television Has Transformed Sports.* Free Press.

Real, M. (2014). Theorizing the Sports-Television Dream Marriage: Why Sports Fit Television So Well. In A. Billings (Ed.), *Sports Media: Transformation, Integration, Consumption* (pp. 19–39). Routledge.

Reyes, L. (2020). NFL Data Shows Concussions Increased Slightly in 2019, But League Touts "New Benchmark." *USAToday.com.* www.usatoday.com/story/sports/nfl/2020/01/23/nfl-concussions-increased-slightly-2019-season/4555094002/

Rowe, D. (2014). Sports Media: Beyond Broadcasting, Beyond Sports, Beyond Societies? In A. Billings (Ed.), *Sports Media: Transformation, Integration, Consumption* (pp. 94–113). Routledge.

Sandvoss, C. (2003). *A Game of Two Halves: Football, Television and Globalization.* Routledge.

Sasuly, R. (1982). *Bookies and Bettors: Two Hundred Years of Gambling.* Holt, Rinehart and Winston.

Siegel, B. (2019). Concussions and Capital: Tom Brady, CTE, and the NFL's Crisis of Identity. *Journal of Sport and Social Issues*, 43(6), 551–574.

Sloop, J. (2012). "This Is Not Natural": Caster Semenya's Gender Threats. *Critical Studies in Media Communication*, 29(2), 81–96.

Spencer, N. (2003). "America's Sweetheart" and "Czech-Mate": A Discursive Analysis of the Evert-Navratilova Rivalry. *Journal of Sport & Social Issues*, 27, 18–37.

Sullivan, D. (2006). Broadcast Television and the Game of Packaging Sports. In A. Raney & J. Bryant (Eds.), *Handbook of Sports and Media* (pp. 131–1146). Routledge.

Tremblay, S. & Tremblay, W. (2001). Mediated Masculinity at the Millennium: The Jim Rome Show as a Male Bonding Speech Community. *Journal of Radio Studies*, 8(2), 271–291.

Vogan, T. (2011). Hard Knocks. *Journal of Sport History*, 38(2), 292–293.

Vogan, T. (2014). *Keepers of the Flame: NFL Films and the Rise of Sports Media.* University of Illinois Press.

Vogan, T. (2015). *ESPN: The Making of a Sports Media Empire.* University of Illinois Press.

Vogan, T. (2018). Exhibiting Ali's "Super Fights": The Contested Politics and Brief History of Closed Circuit Boxing Broadcasts. *Film History*, 30(3), 1–31.

Wanta, W. (2006). The Coverage of Sports in Print Media. In A. Raney & J. Bryant (Eds.), *Handbook of Sports and Media* (pp. 105–116). Routledge.

Wood, C. & Benigni, V. (2006). The Coverage of Sports on Cable TV. In A. Raney & J. Bryant (Eds.), *Handbook of Sports and Media* (pp. 147–170). Routledge.

2
REPRESENTING LIVE AND REAL COMPETITION

As we've seen, the sports/media industries attempt to be ubiquitous and infuse themselves into the lives of sports fans. When successful, this means that fans are regularly in contact with sports media and constantly engaged with its dominant meanings. For example, a fan could wake up and immediately check the previous day's events on the ESPN mobile application. Then, while driving to work, she might listen to sports radio or sports podcasts. Throughout the work day, she checks social media and finds sports news updates. Then, upon returning home, she watches a sports debate show and catches a game broadcast. In this way, the life of a sports fan becomes intertwined with the messages sent by sports media.

After considering some of the industrial forces that shape and profit from the sports genre, we can turn to the texts that are created by these forces. In this chapter, we will focus on the relationship between the generic expectation of live and real competitions and hegemonic ideologies commonly instantiated throughout sports media. The two buoy each other by giving credence to each other. Common messages sent through sports media are naturalized by the feeling of liveness and realness. Indeed, in many cases, live sports can seem like a scientific testing ground in which hegemonic ideologies are validated; for example, the notions that certain races, genders, or body types are more capable for sports are ostensibly proven through competition. The gender and racial makeup of the NFL or the popularity of the NBA over the WNBA can be given as grounds to support sexist and racist tropes.

As discussed in the previous chapter, the genre of sports has been constructed by the sports/media industries. Sports and sports media organizations construct live and real competition to distinguish it from other entertainment options. This project is aided by the hegemony of the messages sent through sports media. If

DOI: 10.4324/9781003164272-3

the power and pervasiveness of hegemonic ideologies seem immutable, and sports media reproduce those ideologies, then sports media will appear to be representing things as they "really are." Sports would seem to present the world as we expect to see it. Sports media's representation of hegemonic ideologies seems to capture realness live. Therefore, the genre of sports and hegemonic ideologies support each other.

This chapter will explore the connection between sports and ideologies by further examining the particularities of the generic conventions of sport. Due to the expectation of physical competition (Suits, 1988), athletes' bodies in competition creates boundaries that enforce hierarchies. As Brian Pronger (1998) notes, these boundaries include distinctions between "man and woman; heterosexual and homosexual; white and 'other'; healthy and sick; animal, human and machine; legitimate play and illicit sex; rationality and irrationality; order and chaos" (pp. 277–278). Though Pronger argues that sports can also be a site for transgression, this chapter will focus on how the genre of sports reinforces and is reinforced by hegemonic ideologies. The literature on representation of identity in sports media is well developed and has been exploding the myth that "sport is an innocent pastime that exists outside the realm of economic and political forces." Scholars of sports representation have advanced "our understandings of race, class, gender, and sexuality by reconceptualizing these identities not as categoric variables but as relations of power" (Birrell & McDonald, 2000, p. 5).

In particular, this chapter will examine how these regularly occurring and powerful ideologies are intertwined with the distinctive genre of sports. This chapter will be divided into three sections that track the three pillars of Suits's (1988) expectations of sport. First, it will foreground the notion of competition itself—that it is a proving ground in which the most talented and prepared succeed. Sports are thought to be a pure competitive space and therefore get associated with notions of fairness, meritocracy, and escapism. Indeed, sports are set up as a sort of "magic circle" (Huizinga, 2014) in which societal and political influences are eliminated. Therefore, only the competition matters. Without outside influences, sports are supposed to determine who is best. In the second section, we will explore how sports are expected to be physical. That is, unlike some games that can be viewed as passive or unathletic, sports are described as active and athletic. There is, therefore, an emphasis on the body. In particular, this section will focus on how the competitive nature of sports creates and supports ideological hierarchies of bodies based on gender, race, ability, and sexuality. Finally, the third section will attend to the idea that competition essentially involves opposition. Including two or more competitors creates an in- and out-group, each infused with notions of class, place, and nationality. Ultimately, this chapter seeks to explore how specific expectations of sports as a physical competition based on opposition create the impression that hegemonic ideologies are real because they are given live epistemic support.

The "Purity" of Live and Real Competition

Viewers expect sport to create a space of pure competition. The GSM is an expression of this concept, defined as the "belief in the inherent purity and goodness of sport" (Coakely, 2015, p. 403). The GSM sets up a dichotomy about what is good and natural in sports and what is corrupt and foreign. What counts as part of sport—and therefore gets to be considered "good" and "normal"—is extremely broad. In fact, it could encompass many parts of a diverse sports/media complex, including aspects that are extremely removed from the actual playing of sports.

Take, for example, the notions of player salaries for professional sports. Being able to pay athletes attracts talent, which increases a team's chances of winning. In this way, monetary payment gets attached to the goodness of sporting competition. Competition and money become linked when professional front offices are praised or critiqued for their player contracts or trades, when players are analyzed for whether they are performing according to their economic worth, and when team owners are commended or condemned for how they spend money. This isn't to say, however, that the connection between labor compensation and sports is always a comfortable one; fans and media members will occasionally critique some teams for their ability and willingness to outspend other teams and essentially buy wins. For example, George Steinbrenner, owner of the New York Yankees from 1973 until his death in 2010, was known to bring in big-name free agents to win. His Yankees were dubbed the "Evil Empire" in the early 2000s due to their success in the late 1990s. The reference to *Star Wars* makes sense, as they were *evil* because this was deemed as unsporting. They were an *empire* because they had the resources to buy star players like Tino Martinez, Wade Boggs, Tim Raines, Darryl Strawberry, Cecil Fielder, and Dwight Gooden (for their 1996 team). This censuring condemns the Yankees for being unsporting with their economic resources. Money can align with the GSM if it falls within agreed-upon constructions of fairness.

The fit between paying a labor force (or not) and the GSM can also be seen in collegiate sports. Because colleges don't pay their athletes, the GSM is often associated with notions of amateurism, in which athletes play for the love of the game or for their college (Oates & Vogan, 2014, p. 329). In this conception, "amateurism is the original, pure state of sport" (Pope, 1996). This discourse is encouraged and constructed by the NCAA and its media partners like CBS. For example, Thomas Oates and Travis Vogan (2014) explore how the end-of-tournament video montage *One Shining Moment* "reinforce[s] the amateur ideal of collegiate sport in an age of increasingly obvious commercialism" (p. 331). The "highlight offers a montage that loosely traces the tournament from its opening rounds through the championship" that portrays "images of players celebrating after wins," "coaches sulking after losses," and "fans widely cheering as . . . saccharine lyrics emphasize teams' efforts to seize the opportunity for greatness"

40 Representing Live and Real Competition

FIGURE 2.1 A college basketball player is shown being comforted by the opposing coach during the end-of-tournament montage of *One Shining Moment* in order to highlight the passion and emotion of the tournament.

(Oates & Vogan, 2014, p. 333). The video foregrounds the passion of players, while ignoring or downplaying the rampant commercialism of the tournament (Figure 2.1). Just as with professional sports, the GSM can be called into question under certain circumstances. For example, when CBS switched the singer of *One Shining Moment* from Luther Vandross to Jennifer Hudson, her version was derided due to claims of her version being inappropriately commercial (Oates & Vogan, 2014). Incursions against amateurism and the GSM show us that these are expected as the default in NCAA sports and that those perceived incursions are due to the apparent changing of tradition.

A related debate is unfolding around the recent decision to allow college athletes to profit from their Name, Image, and Likeness (NIL). Some sports commentators, fans, and politicians condemn athletes for making money off their own NIL as an attack on the purity of collegiate amateurism. At the time of writing this book, the consequences of this policy are still working themselves out, but idealized notions of past amateurism are being leveraged against it. These discourses ignore the ways that money has always been a part of collegiate athletics; it has been present in scholarships, academic support, athletic facilities and resources, and coaching staffs. Money has always been used to gain an upper hand on the field and attract skilled athletes. Because these connections to money have been normalized, they are ignored as infringements upon the GSM and the purity of amateurism. Since amateurism is "more of an ideological construct than an actual set of practices and agreed-upon rules" (Pope, 1996, p. 301), any policy or practice will be judged on ideological grounds.

Whether the GSM is mixed with professionalism or amateurism, it marks sports as pure because of their connection to meritocracy. Sports, since they are games, set up artificial boundaries to be overcome, which determine specific skills relevant for overcoming them (Suits, 1988). Even if those boundaries specify skills that are judged by others as being closer to an ideal (as in gymnastics or ice skating) whether they set the boundaries for a scored competition (as in basketball or football), the sport becomes an opportunity to see who best exercises their skills (Suits, 1988). Judges of sports like gymnastics and ice skating are supposed be impartial in their skill evaluation, and the standard of referees of basketball and football is to apply the rules uniformly to all competitors. Despite the fact that there are moments when referees' judgments are called into question, sports operate on the assumption of the impartiality of a level-playing field. Any other advantages (like home field advantage) or elements of luck (such as the bounce of the ball) are taken to be part of the game. Since these structures determine a winner, it appears that they demonstrate which competitor uses their skills best to overcome the same set of artificial barriers. That is, they appear to provide a definite answer of which competitor has more merit.

The connection to merit is a pillar of the construction of sports' purity. Meritocracy "refers to a social system as a whole in which individuals get ahead and earn rewards in direct proportion to their individual efforts and abilities" (McNamee & Miller, 2009, p. 2). This notion is tied to the American Dream (McNamee & Miller, 2009, p. 2) and is also present in sports. Because of this association, sports are supposed to reflect the meritocratic nature of the United States in a distilled form. The idea that people get what they deserve according to their merit essentially involves the notion of inequality; some people end up with more than others. However, instead of being the result of social and institutional inequities, "[a]ccording to the ideology of meritocracy, inequality is seen to be fair because everyone presumably has an equal (or at least an adequate) chance to succeed, and success is determined by individual merit" (McNamee & Miller, 2009, p. 4).

Despite the fact that athletic resources might not be as readily available to the less affluent, sports get attached to meritocratic discourses both on and off the field. For example, on the field we see discourses about the "magic circle" of playing and gaming, as described earlier. Off-the-field discourses, however, involve the notion that highly visible athletes are often taken as examples of upward social mobility (McNamee & Miller, 2009, p. 29). Such underdog or "rags to riches" stories are common in sports. Because this ideology renders losers invisible (Serazio, 2019, p. 249), it highlights only those who had success. The very American message is that through sports it is possible for anyone with merit to transcend their socioeconomic situation, and those who are don't "are to blame for their chosen indolence" (Serazio, 2019, p. 241).

The notion of sports as escapism is a corollary of meritocratic ideologies. Because sports are supposed to be apolitical and meritocratic, it represents a break from politics and everyday life. Unlike, say, a job in which a worker might feel that people get promoted due to cronyism, sports allegedly levels out inequities, as the best competitors win. Viewed in this way, sports are "our pop culture palliative, our nightly consolation for suffering, by day, the slings and arrows of outrageous fortune" (Serazio, 2019, p. 230). The magic circle extends beyond the sporting competition and into places where fans and audiences engage with sports. The result is an entire complex that is set up to censure athletes when they engage in political speech that violates meritocratic ideologies (see Chapter 3). Coaches, athletes, journalists, commentators, and fans will all censure athletes who supposedly violate their apolitical and meritocratic escape from reality.

The related notions of meritocracy and escapism have been established as inevitable in sports (Serazio, 2019, p. 249). Part of the reason for their naturalization is because they are found throughout the sports media complex (Serazio, 2019, p. 240–248), a saturation enabled by the genre of live and real competition. As noted earlier, real competition is supposed to be a process by which the cream rises to the top. Therefore, the liveness of the real competition exudes a feeling of an empirical testing ground. These purported experiments seem to prove the validity not just of the merit of the winners but also of the apological meritocracy itself. Other genres of entertainment might express these values, but sports' intimate connection to live and real competition makes it a uniquely salient product for the values' expression.

Live and Real Bodies

Sports competitions are held to be physical, which drives debates in stadia, living rooms, and bars. What activities are physical and athletic enough to be considered a "sport?" Golf literally looks like a walk in a park, and NASCAR is a race in which the driver turns only left. Darts and bowling are activities that can be played while drinking beer, and esports can be critiqued as childish diversions. However, supporters could argue that all these activities require dexterity, stamina, concentration, and training that only the elite can achieve. These debates demonstrate that physicality is assumed to be part of sports. Whether playing golf, car racing, throwing darts, bowling, or competing at esports, athletes demonstrate that physicality is taken to be a necessary condition to be considered a sport. Because physicality is a property of athletic activity, our attention in sports is drawn to the athletes' bodies.

This section will explore the conditions in which bodies are represented as athletic or physical. While writing about fantasy sports, Munene Mwaniki (2017) advances a notion of "biological fandom," which normalizes athletes' value as determined by statistics, medical information, and quantification of their bodies. Fantasy sports are a helpful lens from which to motivate the concept, because they are management games in which players must determine which athletes to select

FIGURE 2.2 The hand width of the NFL's Odell Beckham Jr. is measured and displayed on ESPN's *Sport Science*, thereby marking it as noteworthy.

for their team and who to start during the game. The essential strategy of fantasy is to determine which athletes will score more points for one's team. Their value is therefore tied to aspects of their competitive performance. Mwaniki (2017) rightfully notes that biological fandom exists within a broader context, in which sports media enable and encourage this kind of fannish engagement. Therefore, a bodily focus happens throughout the sports/media complex and not just in fantasy games (Figure 2.2). In fact, sports are prominent sites in which a bodily gaze is cast on men (Johnson, 2021, p. 65; Oates, 2017, pp. 54–93). As with fantasy sports, sporting teams and organizations decide who will compete and how much money the athlete will be offered for their competitive performance. Media companies publicize and comment on the worth of players, and fans participate in the debate of who should be selected and is deserving of a high salary. These debates are framed by previous performances and probabilistic reasoning about the future, which, as Mwaniki (2017) reminds us, is constantly being informed by biological and statistical analysis; which bodies are more likely to succeed, prone to injury, or will retain their value for a set amount of time? Which bodies are viewed as having value and what are the resulting hierarchies of valuing them?

Even though the notion of biological and mathematical analysis seems to offer an objective and unbiased way of answering these questions, there are two important points to keep in mind. First, the sports/media complex extends way beyond activities that occur during competition. It follows that athletes' values will never solely be determined by their bio-value and (potential) competitive performance. Grabbing headlines, selling jerseys, and servicing fans can all factor into the decision about who will join an organization. Second, even when the focus is solely placed on competitive value, which kinds of athletic performances are evaluated are thoroughly ideological (Oates, 2017, pp. 17–18). Indeed, sports media "explicitly references race, gender, age, sexuality, and regional 'difference' in ways that appear 'safely' displaced onto the field of play but that, effectively, represented the shared, ritual site for significant interrogation of these culturally constructed categories" (Johnson, 2021, p. 3).

Therefore, any cursory glance at the most popularized sports and sports media outlets will reveal a usual erasure of women and women's athletics. Sports are most commonly associated with men and represented as a space for men (Dworkin & Wachs, 2000, p. 252)—a homosocial enclave "where men police the boundaries of masculinity and express solidarity" (Oates, 2017, p. 27, citing Amanda Lotz's [2014] work on television and masculinity). However, not all performances are equally well received, highlighted, and celebrated by the sports/media complex. Indeed, there is a "valorization of a highly stylized version of traditional masculinity in sports media [that] also expresses and reinforces hegemonic models of manhood while marginalizing alternative masculinities" (Sabo & Jansen, 1992, p. 179). The hegemonic masculinity valorized in sports might not be common, even in sports, because only a "minority of men might enact it" (Cornell & Messerschmidt, 2005, p. 832). Hegemonic masculinity has at least five characteristics: (1) physical force and control, (2) occupational achievement, (3) familial patriarchy, (4) frontiersmanship, and (5) heterosexuality (Trujillo, 1991, p. 291). Women aren't celebrated in sports due to hegemonic masculinity. It is thought that they can't or don't satisfy the five characteristics and therefore aren't worthy of attention.

Because of hegemonic masculinity, women and women's sports are regularly demeaned and ignored by mainstream sports media. Even when men and women are competing in the same sports at the same time, men's sports get more coverage. For example, consider the Olympics (Burch et al., 2012) and NCAA basketball tournaments (Hallmark & Armstrong, 1999), in which the men received more attention. Furthermore, when women's sports are covered, gendered tropes are used because they are thought to attract viewer attention. For example, in sports like golf, tennis, skating, and gymnastics, there are marketing pressures to present women athletes as slim, sexy, and feminine (Creedon, 1998). Instead of focusing on the athletes' power and control—the first marker of hegemonic masculinity—women are sold by being marked as feminine. When presented in this way, the value of women's sports derives from their sexualization and not athleticism. Their physicality is framed for the pleasure of heterosexual men and not regarded as a source of power and control. In a domain in which hegemonic masculinity is taken to be the epitome of physicality, women's bodies and sports are demeaned.

Other bodies are particularly ill-suited for commodification according to hegemonic beauty standards and the male gaze. Women of color, especially when they are dominant in their sport or present in "unfeminine" ways, are marked as unsuitable objects for heterosexual male attention. Take, for example, coverage of basketball player Brittney Griner; media framed her as a tall woman with a long reach that enabled her to block shots and dunk (Lavelle, 2014). These capabilities marked her as having the masculine traits of power, control, and occupational achievement. In other words, she was represented as unfeminine. Her "masculinity" was lauded as special and was used to degrade "normal" women athletes, and it led to rumors about her gender identity (Lavelle, 2014, p. 125). Similar tropes were used to cover track athlete Caster Semenya, in which her "unfeminine" presentation and athletic performance led to doubts about her gender (Sloop, 2012). The coverage of both athletes accords with controlling images of Black women. While some tropes represent Black women as hypersexual, many mark them as unsuitable for straight white male sexual attention (Hill Collins, 2000). Either women are viewed as appropriately feminine and worthy of sexual attention, or unsexual and worthy of simultaneous praise and suspicion for being masculine. Constructions of appropriate performances of race and gender are highlighted when a bodily gaze is turned onto the athletes.

The liveness and realness of the competition reinforce and are reinforced by raced and gendered hierarchies. The idea that women's athletic and physical achievements are less impressive than men's is supported through the notion of competition. To return to Griner's case, the idea that only she might be able to compete with men due to her size and ability to dunk is offered as evidence that women's basketball generally is less worthy than men's (Lavelle, 2014). This is supposedly revealed through competition—no women are in the NBA and few women play like NBA athletes. It is putatively through the real competition that we see that women's sports have less merit than men's, which is given apparently live epistemic support. However, the ideological hierarchies also support the apparent realness and liveness of the sports competition by giving people what they expect to see. The sports/media complex's demeaning of women and women's sports is supported by and reflective of broader misogynistic ideologies.

The distinction between men's and women's sports also upholds the gender binary—the view that there are only two genders. Sports support this ideology by institutionally organizing around gender; there are men's and women's sports and leagues, and even sports that mix genders still instill barriers between them. For example, the UFC arranges men's and women's fights. Furthermore, while the Crossfit Games have competitions in which men and women compete as teams, there are rules about how many men and women are on each team (Figure 2.3). Many sports reinforce and are reinforced by the gender binary. Not only do they offer a clear distinction between the genders to arrange hierarchies, but they also erase the wider gender spectrum. Gender nonconforming and genderqueer individuals are eliminated from hegemonic sports discourses.

FIGURE 2.3   During the Crossfit Games, athletes who compete in a mixed-gender team of four are still strictly divided along gender lines: two men and two women.

The gender binary is upheld by views that gender is essential and immutable (Butler, 1987), which especially harms transgender athletes. In particular, the

> question of [transgender women] competing with cis women is an increasingly important one [because] as trans women begin winning, the broader sporting community debates the fairness and safety of sporting competitions for cis women and the right of trans women to compete.
>
> *(Fischer & McClearen, 2020, p. 148)*

In these debates, we see essentialist notions of the gender binary infused with the misogynistic view of women's sports. Mia Fischer and Jennifer McClearen (2020) examine these notions through Fallon Fox, a transgender woman and mixed martial arts fighter. In a fight with a cis gender woman, if Fox wins, this is proof of her "assumed innate physical superiority awarded at birth" (Fischer & McClearen, 2020, p. 149). Therefore, it seems she must "lose against women to be considered sufficiently female, that is, just as biologically inferior to men as other cis women" (Fischer & McClearen, 2020, p. 148). The assumptions at work are that gender is biological, there are only two genders, and that one is superior to the other. A win by Fox is read as competitive proof that hegemonic assumptions are valid. However, a loss could be evidence that Fox is "sufficiently female," which reifies the gender binary and hierarchy by assuming that Fox is close enough to being a woman to be allowed to compete against cis women. Furthermore, that there's more concern about transgender men athletes than transgender women demonstrates the essentialist hierarchy around sport and gender. Similarly, gender testing policies in other sports like Olympic track and field and gymnastics (Sloop, 2012) are always reserved for women and justify the invasive policies that surveil their bodies.

Masculinity and femininity are multidimensional and it is worth considering how factors beyond gender inform hierarchies of competition. Sexuality, as we saw from Trujillo's (1991) five conditions, also plays a crucial role in constructing masculinity and femininity. While it is possible to have alternative masculinities (Halberstam, 1998), hegemonic masculinity is usually reserved for certain men. The proscription of heterosexuality is foisted on men, so male heterosexuality sets the bar for inclusion or exclusion from masculinity. Sexuality and masculinity both inform each other, and exclusion from one often means exclusion from the other. Using a case study of Mike Piazza of MLB, Michael Butterworth (2006) explores how the perception that Piazza didn't perform masculinity properly buoyed rumors that he was gay. Just as speculation about his sexuality propagated, critique of the passiveness of his on-field performance also circulated (Butterworth, 2006). Both discourses undercut his status as hegemonically masculine; his supposed passivity foreclosed upon power and control, and the gay rumors undercut the demand for heterosexuality. This case is in conversation with a wider history, as Evan Brody (2019) helpfully puts it, of "gay male sports figures whose accomplishments were minimized and/or ignored, such as Emile Griffith and Glenn Burke, because their transgressive bodies prevented them from attaining traditional success" (p. 297). Despite the presence of Pride nights in stadia and sports organizations' celebrations of Pride Month, men's sports still depend on selling hegemonic masculinity and therefore also heterosexuality.

Other bodily scripts, such as racial ones, can inform inclusion or exclusion from hegemonic masculinity. Since hegemonic masculinity is coded as white, many representations of people of color are excluded. Michael Park (2014) explores how the success of Jeremy Lin, an Asian American NBA player, was represented. Lin's dominance in the NBA could have been explained through the norms of hegemonic masculinity like power and control, occupational achievement, and frontiersmanship. Instead it was framed with tropes about Asian and Asian American men as shy, passive, and nerdy—which signifies "a weak and feminine masculinity" (Park, 2014, p. 5). It follows that his ascendancy had to be explained using other means. Media coverage defaulted to other tropes about Asians and Asian Americans to explain how Lin overcame the low expectations that were applied to him; the Asian work ethic, education, and deceptiveness were all used to account for his success (Park, 2014). Examples like Lin's highlight the ideological nature of sports' evaluation of athletes' bodies, their physicality, and their deeds. If any on-court performance could be portrayed as a hegemonically masculine feat, it was Lin's during his 2012 "Linsanity" string of success. However, because of his race, other tropes were applied.

Instead of objective evaluation through sport competition, both the attribution of hegemonic masculinity and the lack of attribution are based on social constructs. Different tropes—and therefore different ways of being included or excluded from hegemonic masculinity—can come to the forefront depending on factors, like the how athletes present themselves and compete. Take, for instance, Justin García's (2013) analysis of the coverage of Oscar De La Hoya and Fernando Vargas. These two successful Mexican American boxers were portrayed and read in very different ways. Vargas was known for his ferocious, aggressive, and offensive fighting style (García, 2013, p. 334) and was framed as adopting a "warrior style" associated with Mexican and Mexican American boxers (García, 2013, p. 330). By being Mexican American and fighting in a certain fashion, Vargas was framed as "manly" (García, 2013, p. 329). By contrast, De La Hoya was portrayed as eschewing "the warrior brand of fighting popularity associated with Mexican and Mexican American fighters, opting for a much more tactical and cautious style of fighting" (García, 2013, p. 330). The appraisal of his tactics inside the ring was supposedly substantiated by his reception and activities outside of the ring. His attractiveness was highlighted in news coverage and his advertisements, which drew in heterosexual women fans (García, 2013, p. 330). Yet De La Hoya was characterized as "cowardly, gay, and effeminate" (García, 2013, p. 332). It is consistent with the coverage of Piazza that an alleged violation of one component of hegemonic masculinity (power and control) led to an undermining of others (heterosexuality). De La Hoya and Vargas remind us that hegemonic masculinity is a fragile complex of attributes. Even for athletes in a combat sport, being represented as hegemonically masculine is constantly in peril.

Because hegemonic masculinity is a normative ideal that very few (if any) live up to, it follows that disqualification is always threatening. However, we've seen that, based on gender, sexuality, and race/ethnicity, some groups' inclusion is more tenuous than others. Even with the stereotype of the Mexican warrior style of boxing, De La Hoya and Vargas were expected to perform their sport and ethnicity to accord with hegemonic masculinity. De La Hoya didn't and was critiqued for it, and Vargas was accepted as long as he continued to act in hegemonically masculine ways. Because hegemonic masculinity is coded as white and is fragile, all athletes of color must continually embody it to be included. Richard Mocarski and Andrew Billings (2014) make this point with respect to LeBron James. Even though Black athletes are associated with strength and speed (Oates, 2017, pp. 17–18), other negative stereotypes—like being connected to drugs, violence, cheating, selfishness, and laziness—threaten their inclusion in white notions of hegemonic masculinity (Grano, 2010). LeBron James and his sponsor Nike, therefore, had to present an image of the athlete that distanced "his brand from these negative associations of Blackness, while embracing the positive associations" with hegemonic masculinity (Mocarski & Billings, 2014, p. 6). Walking this tightrope involved associating James with Trujillo's (1991) five aspects of hegemonic masculinity. Even for a superstar like James playing a physical game like basketball, his inclusion in hegemonic masculinity was conditional and needed to be constantly maintained.

The linking of hegemonic masculinity to bodies in sports highlights bodily difference according to common ideologies. Parasports—sports played by people with disabilities—are another point at which this ideological linkage becomes clear. Despite that "disability is much richer, more complex, and more present in everyday life than is generally realized" (Ellis & Goggin, 2015, p. 2) and that the concept is so complex that it is difficult to parse the categories of people with disabilities and people without disabilities (Ellis & Goggin, 2015, p. 6), just as with the gender binary, a physical activity is *either* a sport or a parasport. In other words, disability too is a binary rife with normativity. Parasports are demeaned to the point that it is held to be an "ideological paradox" to even have people with disabilities compete in sports (Hardin, 2006, p. 578). Parasports, therefore, are covered less than other sports (Hardin, 2006, p. 581) but also contain tropes not found elsewhere. Take, for instance, "the supercrip model, which emphasizes the person with a disability as overcoming a disability to lead a normal life" that enables the person to do something athletic like climb Mt. Everest (Hardin, 2006, p. 582). This model assumes "that people with disabilities are pitiful (and useless), until they overcome their disabilities through rugged individualism and pull off a feat considered heroic by the mainstream" (Hardin, 2006, p. 582). Like the aforementioned Griner case, individual praise often devalues parasports generally. While analysis needs to address carefully the sport and abilities of the athletes (e.g., see Goggin & Newell, 2000), many parasports are demeaned simply because the athletes' physicality looks different from hegemonic masculinist expectations (Hardin, 2006).

It is also worth considering the role that the sports themselves play in the portrayal of the physicality of athletes' bodies. Indeed, "distinctive identities are assigned to particular sports" (Oates, 2017, p. 6). Sports don't exist in a vacuum and have been (as we saw in Chapter 1) constructed to be entertaining and commodifiable products. For example, the physicality and speed of collegiate and professional football have slowly developed over time (Chandler, 1988). But it is also important to keep in mind that scripts about particular sports exist *within* the tropes discussed earlier. Sports like basketball and football are held to be "masculine appropriate" (Dworkin & Wachs, 2000, p. 252) and a "fortress of masculinity" (Oates, 2017, p. 26). The NBA and NFL have constructed their products to involve strength and quickness and rely on tropes of strength and speed associated with their labor force consisting largely of Black men. Contrast this with sports such as women's tennis, golf, figure skating, and gymnastics, in which the athletes' physicality are framed using "feminine" attributes like "self-sacrifice, glamour, and grace" (Baroffio-Bota & Banet-Weiser, 2006, p. 487). Without the regular interpersonal contact of a sport like football, there is opportunity for women athletes in these sports to have their physicality downplayed. It isn't just how women's sports are covered that marks them as different from men's, but it is also sometimes the way the sport has been constructed. There is, of course, men's tennis, golf, figure skating, and gymnastics, and women's basketball and football—which also import assumptions about masculinity and femininity. Furthermore, even the way that the same sport is constructed can contain gendered assumptions, such as in high-level ice hockey in which men are allowed to body check and women commonly are not. Physical contact gives the opportunity for men's hockey to seem more physical and masculine. Therefore, the sports themselves set the conditions in which athletes' bodies are viewed and evaluated.

Even though hegemonic masculinity is a marker in the sports/media complex of being athletic, interesting, and profitable, it is thoroughly informed by racist, sexist, homophobic, transphobic, and ableist ideologies. Due to sports' focus on physicality and bodies, these ideologies support and are supported by the apparent liveness and realness of competition. Competition gives the impression that certain bodies are better suited for the physicality of sport. This is because sports offer what is expected due to the fact that they follow hegemonic ideologies. In this way, the realness of sports is substantiated because it contains these ideologies, but the ideologies are also demonstrated through live and real competition. Sports' focus on bodily competition offers a particularly powerful site at which hegemonic hierarchies are reinforced.

Live and Real Opposition

The expectation of physical competition involves opposition. Because sports are set up to result in winners and losers, competitors are positioned against each other. This oppositional aspect of sports lends itself to the notion that sports reveal merit-based hierarchies. The nature of opposition depends on the sport. Sports like singles tennis or boxing involve two athletes directly competing. Sports like baseball or soccer match two teams against each other. Golf and racing sports like Formula 1 pit an entire field of competitors against each other; the former does so indirectly by seeing who can play the course better, and the latter does so directly by having drivers drive the same track simultaneously. Individual games, matches, and races can also take place in the context of a broader competition; each MLB team plays 162 games for the chance to make the playoffs and win the World Series, UFC competitors can engage in multiple fights to attempt to win a Championship Belt, and F1 drivers race multiple times to accumulate the most points and win the World Drivers' Championship. Even though there are many ways to arrange the competition of sport, opposition remains a core component that manifests in sports media texts.

Sports leagues and organizations set the terms for and mark the importance of opposition. For example, regular season games determine which competitors make the playoffs, which then establish who might win the championship. Which competitors play each other, when it happens, where it happens, and why audiences should care are often determined by sports leagues and are echoed by sports media. In this context, fans also help construct and expect opposition. The notion of "oppositional fandom" (Lopez & Lopez, 2017) captures how opposition is a crucial part of the genre of sports. It is formulated by sports/media industries and fans and therefore is also present throughout sports media texts.

Opposition in the sports/media complex involves dramatic narratives, such as in sports movies. Both biographical and fictional films commonly highlight opposition through competition. Movies like *Hoosiers* and *Rocky* fictionalize opposition in real sports, and *Rollerball* and *BASEketball* reference opposition in made-up sports. Fictionalized sports stories can span genre and includes children's movies like *The Mighty Ducks*, *The Sandlot*, and *Space Jam*, to comedy in *Major League*, *Slap Shot*, and *Happy Gilmore*, and sci-fi in *Death Race 2000*, *Speed Racer*, and *The Running Man*. Sports biographies also highlight competition; *Rudy* highlights the final game of a football season, *Miracle* the 1980 US Olympic hockey team's win over the Soviet Union's, and *Ali* 1974's *Rumble in the Jungle* against George Foreman. This isn't to say, however, that every sports film is premised on a big game or even focuses on sporting competition. *Moneyball* and *Draft Day* are more about sports management than opposition through games. Still, telling a story of competitive opposition through sports is a hallmark of sports films narratives.

The fact that opposition lends itself so easily to storytelling in sports shows that ideology shapes how the opposition is understood. A starting place for understanding the ideological underpinning of opposition is through the basic notion that competitions pit two or more sides against each other. Whether it is an individual, a team, or a field sport, factions are created—and usually only one can win. When combined with the notion of meritocracy, it follows that the better and/or more deserving competitors tend to win. A victory over one's opponent means one is more deserving, capable, and/or virtuous. In this way, sporting opposition enacts normativity. However, as we've seen, who is the better or more worthy competitor is not known with certainty in advance. The epistemic uncertainty of sports generates an open normative question that lingers until the conclusion of the competition; not knowing who will win is correlated with not knowing who is best. There are, of course, competitions in which it is held that one side got lucky or played above their skill level. However, these cases only highlight the assumption that sports opposition is *usually* expected to be connected to normativity, since they are viewed as outliers. A story in which the good side wins is just and one in which the good loses is a tragedy. Ultimately, the narrative links identification with the good and lack of identification with the bad. This allows for "othering" in which the side of good is the familiar "me" or "us" and the other side is the alien "you" or "them."

A binary way of normatively arranging opponents into categories of good/bad and us/them imbues sports with social and political meanings. These meanings are commonly organized around place in sports and, therefore, track social and political ways of codifying place. For this reason, sports often support narratives about nations, states, cities, and communities. From stories about a local kid finding athletic success, to a team representing the pride of an entire country, the opposition in sports creates a geographical in-group. However, to be from one place is not to be from others and therefore a geographical Other is created. This distinction brings political and social ideologies into the oppositional narratives of sport. International sports competitions like the Olympics are powerful sites for using the competitive opposition of sport to communicate ideologies about nations. Whether through athlete representation or overall medal count, countries are a salient category through which narratives about competition are organized. However, in the Olympics, countries are represented as unified wholes, obscuring common discourses about social divisions like race, region, and gender (Hartmann, 2003, p. 17). The result is a competition in which uniform countries oppose each other. Therefore, Olympic competition is an opportunity for whole countries to be compared to each other through opposition.

For example, the 1980 "Miracle on Ice" was infused with political comparisons between the United States and the Soviet Union. As a "metaphor for American resolve and virtue during the Cold War, the [American] team symbolized the superiority of democracy and freedom over [Soviet] communism and totalitarianism" (Butterworth, 2010, p. 134). The meaning of this game, and its ability to paint a picture of the United States through contrast, can be updated for ideological purposes that serve the political moment. Post-9/11, there was a renewed interested in the Miracle on Ice because it was shaped to fit "the heightened patriotism that was central to American identity after 9/11" that, among other things, "was characterized by appeals to fear [and] rigid constructions of 'us' and 'them'" (Butterworth, 2010, p. 135). Indeed, events like the Olympics are powerful opportunities to construct political enemies (Straub, & Overton, 2013). Whether supported by comparisons to specific countries or a vague Other, what it means to be American or an "American patriot" is defined through international competition.

Other sites can support notions of national belonging. For example, pregame performances of the national anthem, especially in NFL games, represent the United States, citizenship, and patriotism. In particular, it creates a spectacle in which being American is associated with support for the US military and its actions (Butterworth, 2014). This spectacle is marked with certain behaviors: standing during the anthem, singing along, flag waving, and chanting "USA." In the space created by the national anthem, those who behave as expected represent patriotic Americans, and those who don't are roundly critiqued for being divisive and un-American. When Colin Kaepernick knelt during the anthem to protest police brutality and social injustice, he was critiqued by many as being "anti-military, anti-American, and divisive" (Lopez, 2021, p. 5). During a spectacle in which patriotism is associated with a certain set of behaviors, any person deciding to deviate is viewed as an outsider, a threat, and an Other.

Events like the Olympics and spectacles like the performance of the national anthem do ideological work when they present countries as unified wholes. Their unification makes countries distinct; if the United States is being celebrated for being a free society without discrimination, then it is implied that other countries don't offer those same freedoms. Not all messages about other countries are this implicit. The opposition of sports often affords the opportunity to compare two places and construct oppositional meanings, which can be seen in sports rivalries. Even though we have seen that most sports involve opposition, rivalries offer particularly regular and stable networks of meanings to analyze. Rivalries, especially long-standing ones, reveal messages about place through juxtaposing the two rivals. Vivi Theodoropoulou (2007) explores this for two Greek soccer rivals: Panathinaikos and Olympiakos. While Theodoropoulou's (2007) work focuses on how rivalries are expressed through fandom, it is acknowledged that fan understandings are informed by the wider sports/media complex (p. 318). That is, the fannish understandings develop as part of a broad set of meanings found throughout sports and media. When one team is understood as "upscale" and the other as "blue-collar" (Theodoropoulou, 2007, pp. 321–322), these scripts pervade fans' understanding of the rivalry. Each team is comprehended in opposition to the other. Theodoropoulou (2007) examines the sociohistorical reasons for these particular scripts and finds that many rivalries involve meanings that extend well beyond competition and sport.

We already saw how pitting the United States against the Soviet Union was imbued with international political tensions, and Theodoropoulou's work reminds us to understand the scripts about the United States in contrast with scripts about the Soviet Union. Scripts are relied on in intranational rivalries; the Los Angeles Lakers and Boston Celtics NBA rivalries of the 1980s were as much about class and race as basketball, for instance. The scope of these oppositional scripts can also account for cross-city rivalries, such as the racial and class-based divide of Chicago being reflected in tropes about MLB's Cubs and White Sox. In rivalries, sports competition becomes a site for the regular expression of oppositional political and social scripts. Because competition is generically understood to be live and real, the winners of those scripts appear to play out through the competition. Will the Hollywood flash of Magic Johnson's Lakers win or will Larry Bird's white- and blue-collar team? These scripts don't need to match the actual composition of the team—Johnson himself came from a working-class background and the Celtics certainly had Black team members—but scripted tensions are imposed on what is supposed to be merely a competition.

It is also common for narratives to revolve less around the opposition of competitors and more around an individual or a team using the competition to overcome their social circumstances. These sports stories commonly tie directly back to the notion of the meritocracy of sport; sports can enable athletes to overcome circumstances like economic hardship or even institutional inequities like racism. Take *Rise*, a biographical film about the NBA star Giannis Antetokounmpo and his family. While Giannis and his brother's success on the court is a part of the story, their family faces unsympathetic immigration policies and harsh poverty. Through the talent and hard work of the brothers, and their family's support, they transcend their situation and make it to the United States, where Giannis is ultimately drafted to the NBA. Even when the opposition on the court is downplayed, sports narratives still regularly use the framing of opposition to highlight the notion of sporting merit.

Conclusion: The Genre-Based Network of Sports Meanings

There is an entire network of meanings commonly associated with the genre of live and real competition. We've seen a reciprocal relationship in this chapter between the hegemonic ideologies found in sports and the sports genre. The apparent realness and liveness of sports gives the sense that the ideologies are real and proven live through competition. It is supposedly through the purity of sport that it is proven that women's sports have less merit; one need only to look at the two kinds of competition and see that women are less physical or athletic than men. However, the support goes the other way too; because sports present people with what they expect to see, sports end up seeming real. For instance, if there are powerful stereotypes that equate Blackness with speed and physicality, then sports appear to be more real when they portray those stereotypes. The genre of sports thus confirms hegemonic ideologies and vice versa.

In the context of live and real competition, a diverse set of meanings are validated by and validate each other. Intersectionality, therefore, must be foregrounded in research on sport. For example, the degradation of femininity—and its corresponding degradation of women, queer folk, and particular racial and ethnic groups—is enmeshed with other scripts about what athleticism and physicality are supposed to look like.

While these associations shift and are always being contested, their connections are also perpetuated throughout sports and sports media and, therefore, validated by the genre of liveness and realness. Regardless of how strong and pervasive these networks of meanings are, they remain constructions that can be altered, albeit with difficulty. Even though some repressive meanings and associations could be replaced with others that are also harmful, sports organizations, media companies, and fans reinterpret and even undermine some of these harmful tropes. We'll see in the following chapters how sports leagues, athletes, and fans can all rewrite hegemonic meanings found in sport.

Bibliography

Baroffio-Bota, D. & Banet-Weiser, S. (2006). Women, Team Sports, and the WNBA: Playing Like a Girl. In A. Raney & J. Bryant (Eds.), *Handbook of Sports and Media* (pp. 485–500). Routledge.

Billings, A. (2014). Reaction Time: Assessing the Record and Advancing a Future of Sports Media Scholarship. In A. Billings (Ed.), *Sports Media: Transformation, Integration, Consumption* (pp. 181–190). Routledge.

Birrell, S. & McDonald, M. (2000). Reading Sport, Articulating Power Lines: An Introduction. In S. Birrell & M. McDonald (Eds.), *Reading Sport: Critical Essays on Power and Representation* (pp. 3–13). Northeastern University Press.

Brody, E. (2019). With the 249th Pick . . .: Michael Sam and Imagining Failure Otherwise. *Journal of Sport and Social Issues*, 43(4), 296–318.

Burch, L., Eagleman, A. & Pederson, P. (2012). New Media Coverage of Gender in the 2010 Winter Olympics: An Examination of Online Media Content. *International Journal of Sport Management*, 13, 143–159.

Butler, J. (1987). Variations on Sex and Gender: Beauvoir, Wittig, Foucault. In S. Benhabib & D. Cornell (Eds.), *Feminism as Critique: Essay on the Politics of Gender in Late Capitalist Societies* (pp. 128–152). Blackwell Publishing.

Butterworth, M. (2006). Pitchers and Catchers: Mike Piazza and the Discourse of Gay Identity in the National Pastime. *Journal of Sport & Social Issues*, 30(2), 138–157.

Butterworth, M. (2010). Do You Believe in Nationalism? American Patriotism in *Miracle*. In H. Hundley & A. Billings (Eds.), *Examining Identity in Sports Media* (pp. 133–152). Sage Publishing.

Butterworth, M. (2014). Public Memorializing in the Stadium: Mediate Sport, the 10th Anniversary of 9/11, and the Illusion of Democracy. *Communication & Sport*, 2(3), 203–224.

Chandler, J. (1988). *Television and National Sport: The United States and Britain*. University of Illinois Press.

Coakely, J. (2015). Assessing the Sociology of Sport: On Cultural Sensibilities and the Great Sport Myth. *International Review for the Sociology of Sport*, 50(4–5), 402–406.

Cornell, R. & Messerschmidt, J. (2005). Hegemonic Masculinity: Rethinking the Concept. *Gender & Society*, 19(6), 829–859.

Creedon, P. (1998). Women, Sport, and Media Institutions: Issues in Sports Journalism and Marketing. In L. Wenner (Ed.), *MediaSport* (pp. 88–99). Routledge.

Dworkin, S. & Wachs, F. (2000). "Disciplining the Body": HIV-Positive Male Athletes, Media Surveillance, and the Policing of Sexuality. *Sociology of Sport Journal*, 15(1), 1–20.

Ellis, K. & Goggin, G. (2015). *Disability and the Media*. Palgrave.

Fischer, M. & McClearen, J. (2020). Transgender Athletes and the Queer Art of Athletic Failure. *Communication & Sport*, 8(2), 147–167.

García, J. (2013). Boxing, Masculinity, and *Latinidad*: Oscar De La Hoya, Fernando Vargas, and *Raza* Representations. *The Journal of American Culture*, 36(4), 323–341.

Goggin, G. & Newell, C. (2000). Crippling Paralympics? Media, Disability and Olympism. *Media International Australia*, 97(1), 71–83.

Grano, D. (2010). Risky Dispositions: Thick Moral Description and Character-Talk in Sports Culture. *Southern Communication Journal*, 75, 255–276.

Gray, J. (2010). *Show Sold Separately: Promos, Spoilers, and Other Media Paratexts*. New York University Press.

Halberstam, J. (1998). *Female Masculinity*. Duke University Press.
Hallmark, J. & Armstrong, R. (1999). Gender Equity in Televised Sports: A Comparative Analysis of Men's and Women's NCAA Division I Basketball Championship Broadcasts, 1991–1995. *Journal of Broadcasting & Electronic Media*, 43(2), 222–235.
Hardin, M. (2006). Disability and Sport: (Non)Coverage of an Athletic Paradox. In A. Raney & J. Bryant (Eds.), *Handbook of Sports and Media* (pp. 577–585). Routledge.
Hartmann, D. (2003). *Race, Culture, and the Revolt of the Black Athlete: The 1968 Olympic Protests and Their Aftermath*. University of Chicago Press.
Hill Collins, P. (2000). *Black Feminist Thought: Knowledge, Consciousness, and the Politics of Empowerment*. Routledge.
Huizinga, J. (2014). *Homo Ludens: A Study of the Play-Element in Culture*. Martino Publishing.
Johnson, V. (2021). *Sports TV*. Routledge.
Lavelle, K. (2014). "Plays like a Guy": A Rhetorical Analysis of Brittney Griner in Sports Media. *Journal of Sports Media*, 9(2), 115–131.
Lopez, J. (2021). Rewriting Activism: The NFL Takes a Knee. *Critical Studies in Media Communication*, 38(2), 183–196.
Lopez, L. & Lopez, J. (2017). Deploying Oppositional Fandoms: Activists' Use of Sports Fandom in the Redskins Controversy. In J. Gray, C. Sandvoss, & C. Harrington (Eds.), *Fandom: Identities and Communities in a Mediated World* (pp. 315–332). New York University Press.
Lotz, A. (2014). *Cable Guys: Television and Masculinities in the 21st Century*. New York University Press.
McClearen, J. (2021). *Fighting Visibility: Sports Media and Female Athletes in the UFC*. University of Illinois Press.
McNamee, S. & Miller, R. (2009). *The Meritocracy Myth*. Rowman & Littlefield.
Mocarski, R. & Billings, A. (2014). Manufacturing a Messiah: Now Nike and Lebron James Co-Constructed the Legend of King James. *Communication & Sport*, 2(1), 3–23.
Mwaniki, M. (2017). Biological Fandom: Our Changing Relationship to Sport and the Bodies We Watch. *Communication & Sport*, 5(1), 49–68.
Oates, T. (2017). *Football and Manliness: An Unauthorized Account of the NFL*. University of Illinois Press.
Oates, T. & Vogan, T. (2014). The Sporting Paratext, Reception, and the Male Domain in CBS's "One Shining Moment." *Communication & Sport*, 2(4), 328–344.
Park, M. (2014). Race, Hegemonic Masculinity, and the "Linpossible!": An Analysis of Media Representations of Jeremy Lin. *Communication & Sport*, 1(23), 1–23.
Pope, S. (1996). Amateurism and American Sports Culture: The Invention of an Athletic Tradition in the United States, 1970–1900. *The International Journal of the History of Sport*, 13(3), 290–309.
Pronger, B. (1998). Post-Sport: Transgressing Culture in Physical Culture. Sport and Post. In G. Rail (Ed.), *Sport and Postmodern Times*. State University of New York Press.
Sabo, D. & Jansen, S. (1992). Images of Men in Sport Media: The Social Reproduction of Gender Order. In S. Craig (Ed.), *Men, Masculinity, and the Media* (pp. 169–184). Sage.
Serazio, M. (2019). *The Power of Sports: Media and Spectacle in American Culture*. New York University Press.
Sloop, J. (2012). "This is Not Natural": Caster Semenya's Gender Threats. *Critical Studies in Media Communication*, 29(2), 81–96.

Straub, S. & Overton, J. (2013). The Symbolic Politics of Olympic Cheating Scandals: Representing International Tensions in Sport. *The International Journal of Sport and Society*, 3, 65–78.

Suits, B. (1988). Tricky Triad: Games, Play, and Sport. *Journal of the Philosophy of Sport*, 9, 1–9.

Theodoropoulou, V. (2007). The Anti-Fan Within the Fan: Awe and Envy in Sport Fandom. In J. Gray, C. Sandvoss, & C. Harrington (Eds.), *Fandom: Identities and Communities in a Mediated World* (pp. 316–327). New York University Press.

Trujillo, N. (1991). Hegemonic Masculinity on the Mound: Media Representation of Nolan Ryan and American Sports Culture. *Critical Studies in Mass Communication*, 8(3), 290–308.

3
LIVE AND REAL ATHLETE EXPRESSION

Some of the most indelible images of political activism come from athletes. Bill Russell, Jim Brown, Kareem Abdul-Jabbar (then Lew Alcindor) flanking Muhammad Ali in support of his rejection of being drafted for the Vietnam War. John Carlos and Tommie Smith's raising their gloved fists during the 1968 Olympics. Mahmoud Abdul-Rauf silently praying with his eyes closed and Colin Kaepernick kneeling during the national anthem. Members of the US Women's National Soccer Team, like Megan Rapinoe, holding interviews and advocating for equal pay. Layshia Clarendon and Breanna Stewart announcing on-court that the 2020 WNBA season would be dedicated to Breonna Taylor.

These images remind us that, so far, we have largely understood real and live sports by analyzing how powerful corporate entities have shaped media messages. It is important to recognize, however, that it is possible to resist them. In this chapter, we'll consider how the athlete labor force can infuse sports media with counter-hegemonic messages and, when the athletes are also famous, can spread them throughout popular culture. In one way, celebrity athletes are like other celebrities; they are highly visible and their actions are broadly analyzed and discussed. However, famous athletes hold powerful influence over the genre of sports. As we've seen, sports leagues and media companies profit from representing their product as live and real competitions, which athletes help construct. Seeing the unscripted performances of athletes play out synchronously generates profit for these companies. Furthermore, as we've also seen, the construction of liveness and realness falls outside of the competition and into non-game and off-season activities. The actions of athletes—both on and off the field—become part of the entertainment product. This attribute of sports media means that athletes—especially celebrity athletes—have the ability to import messages usually foreign

DOI: 10.4324/9781003164272-4

to the sports media complex into that complex. Therefore, sports organizations and companies attempt to limit players' ability to express themselves, while insisting that their in-game identity is authentic.

Movie and television stars can similarly use their platform to speak in ways that their employers might not desire. However, their actions remain removed from on-screen characters and narratives. Paratextual information always informs how people read what is considered the "central" text—like taking an actor's tweet and using that to interpret acting decisions which shape the overall narrative (Gray, 2010)—but sports media sets up no barriers between the mediated athlete and the "real" athlete. While there is a natural distinction between character and actor, which can be traversed with paratexts, nothing similar holds for athletes, due to the expectation of liveness and realness. Sports media constructs the feeling that who the athletes are during the competition is the same as outside of it.

While most sports rely on such imposed realness, other forms of entertainment make use of it as well. Consider how reality television benefits from creating the impression that people on-screen are authentically presenting who they are off-screen. Given the porous nature of generic boundaries, this should be expected. However, the sports genre is constructed in a novel way. While reality TV can claim to capture real events, sports—due to the fairly direct mediation of unscripted competition—maintain that they show what "really happens" live. We've seen that liveness too is a construction, but sports competition—unlike reality TV—aren't prerecorded and edited, which gives it a unique claim.

Liveness and realness captured during games spreads out across sports media. Indeed, the sports and media complex offers further opportunities to speak out on social media or on personally produced documentaries and profiles in an apparently live and real fashion. Coverage of practices, pre- and post-game interviews, and other forms of expression during the competition itself all allow athletes to blend their thoughts with the values and associations of sports media corporations. In fact, it is through sports that white audiences might hear about racial injustice and activism against it (Edwards, 2017, p. 32). In this chapter, we will explore the power struggle between sports institutions and activist athletes; how do leagues shape athlete expression in brand-friendly ways, and how does the athletes' response throughout the sports/media complex imbue the brands with activism?

The Shaping of Athlete Expression

In previous chapters, we saw how the genre of live and real competition helps leagues and media companies distinguish sports as a unique entertainment brand and product. Athletes are the principal pillars of sports products; there would be no sports to watch without the athletes who play them. Competition is based around their performance, which—as we've seen—is structured as being real and as playing out live. Their part in constructing the genre is not, however, limited to competition. Their role goes well beyond how fast they can run, how high they can jump, and how quick their reflexes are. Indeed, the live and real narratives of sports are shaped by what athletes say in pre- and post-game interviews, during press conferences, through advertisements, and on social media. The impression is that fans get to see accurate representations of who the athletes truly are.

The leagues aren't the only entities that benefit from the sense that sports represent athletes as they are. Because brands help organize the intricate relationships between the content-providing leagues, sponsors, labor force, and fans (Lury, 2004), the generic expectations of the leagues' competition-based product reverberate throughout the sports/media complex. Indeed, the leagues are a central node from which others can weave a web of related interests and meanings. Generic expectations focused on the players can be injected into coverage of the leagues by sports media companies like ESPN and Fox Sports, commercials produced by official partners, and even the athletes' brands. The result is an entire complex that makes use of the expectation that sports involve displaying the athletes as they really are.

However, the association with live and real competition isn't the only facet of the leagues' brands and therefore they must juggle other values and associations. The result is a complicated branded network in which each component informs the meanings of the leagues and of each other. Consequently, the generic conventions of sport can't be read on their own; they are also shaped by other aspects of the brand. If, for example, a league brands itself as being patriotic, that value must be represented by live and real athlete expression; athletes must be shown performing patriotism "authentically." This kind of "authentic" expression legitimates the association with patriotism by making it seem live and real, as well as conforms to the generic expectation of liveness and realness.

For their part, athletes can use the opportunities afforded by the leagues to express themselves in ways that undercut other values associated with the leagues' brands. Because of this, athletes represent a double threat to the leagues. First, they can undermine the leagues' particular branded values. But, second, they can weaken the larger branded complex, threatening the overall cohesion of the brand. A serious concern for the leagues emerges from this double threat; expression is a crucial part of their live and real brand, but that free expression runs the risk of contradicting other brand values as well as brand unity.

To mitigate that risk, leagues manage their athletes inside and outside of competition by making practical decisions based on the particularities of their brand and their labor force. Take, for example, the ambivalent relationship between leagues like the NBA and NFL, and their largely Black labor force. Due to the previously mentioned centrality of the players in the leagues' brand-building project, Black athletes are well represented in professional basketball and football. The result is a product that informs and is informed by tropes about Blackness.

The leagues will always be understood in relationship to hegemonic meanings associated with Blackness and, due to sports' construction of physicality, with Black bodily scripts (Chapter 2). The leagues' ambivalence depends on the degree to which these stereotypes can be exploited to attract the leagues' largely white commodity audience, rather than alienate them (Cunningham, 2009; Grainger et al., 2006). For example, the racist tropes that associate Blackness—especially Black masculinity—with criminality and violence threaten the leagues' brand (Cunningham 2009). Throughout their histories, the NBA and NFL have confronted the perception that they were becoming "too Black"—associated with gangs, street culture, and violence. In the 1990s, NBA players like Allen Iverson styled themselves with baggier uniforms, natural hairstyles, and tattoos. Combined with a playing style that included crossovers, which was seen by some to be "street-ball," the NBA was concerned that this would harm their popularity. The NFL had its own versions of when racist tropes threatened its brand, such as a spate of high-profile sexual assault and domestic abuse cases in the 1990s. The worry was that the league would be read as consisting of violent and out-of-control Black men.

The leagues' responses to these cases demonstrate how they shape how their labor force—and therefore their brand—is viewed: through league policies and through media campaigns. Leagues can institute policies that surveil athlete expression and threaten punishment for transgressions. Such surveillance, and therefore what is worthy of sanction by fines or suspensions, can apply both in and out of the competition. The NBA, for example, created rules about how athletes could dress before, during, and after each game (Cunningham, 2009). The NFL enacted policies that could suspend athletes allegedly involved in domestic abuse or sexual assault (Oriard, 2003, p. 195). These kinds of policies have two outcomes for the leagues. First, they attempted to discourage behavior that they thought to be antithetical to their brands. Their strategy was to leverage the players' money and playing time to pressure them to act in certain ways. Second, and maybe more powerfully, these policies communicated to fans that the leagues shared their values and took these issues seriously; the leagues aren't being lost to "uncontrollable thugs" without a fight.

The idea that policies can be a public declaration of the brands' values hints at another path the leagues take when shaping the perception of their labor force. Sports leagues can be thought of as media companies (instead of the classic way of conceiving them merely as content providers) that have curated a media complex of social media, mobile applications, websites, and film. Media campaigns can draw from all of these resources. These transmedia campaigns can work throughout the significant presence of the leagues, including through partners that highlight them during game broadcasts or that sponsor them. Campaigns therefore represent a powerful force in brand-building. While players can show up to events, behave as they please, and release information through their own social media accounts, the leagues have the power to capture, edit, and distribute their own picture of the events and players. Partners and sponsors can support the image, thereby giving it more credibility and visibility.

For example, take the NFL's Salute to Service campaign. Its celebration of the US military and its personnel comes in the form of fundraising, online videos, references during game broadcasts, merchandise, social media hashtags, and partnerships with the United Services Automobile Association. Many of these foreground NFL players and coaches discussing their personal connections to the armed forces and paying homage to military members. Under the campaign, the NFL's coaches, players, teams, and sponsors are represented as being intimately connected to the US military. The players, as the stars of the league, play a crucial part.

Taken together, policies and media campaigns represent powerful ways by which the leagues shape the public perception of their athlete labor force. They both maintain the sense of live and real competition while ensuring that athlete expression is brand-friendly. Policies not only attempt to deter athletes from behaving in ways that violate brand values but also send messages about what the brands value. Media campaigns also do the latter through significantly shaping how the athletes appear. The resulting picture is of athletes acting in an apparently live and real fashion that aligns with the brand.

It is also important to recognize that there are less legitimate ways to handle players who are expressing themselves in ways contrary to the interest of the leagues. The year after Colin Kaepernick knelt on the sidelines to advocate for social and racial justice, he was not rostered by any team and, as of the writing of this book, never played on another team in the NFL. This led some to claim that Kaepernick was being blacklisted by the NFL, and he eventually filed a lawsuit against the NFL claiming as much. While only being alleged, blacklisting is another mechanism, though illicit, that is available for leagues to attempt to silence athletes who behave in ways deemed detrimental to the leagues.

The Limits of the Leagues

While the leagues exert power to influence and shape athlete expression, they encounter significant limitations. First, there are legal limitations like the right to free speech, and being accused of blacklisting athletes who undercut the brand can be a judicial ordeal. For example, the NFL eventually settled Kaepernick's lawsuit. However, even the policies and campaigns of the leagues have limits. Because the leagues benefit from the appearance of live and real athlete expression, athletes' actions infuse league branding with their messages. Athletes have this power because the branding of the leagues is a complex project made up by disparate entities, which can articulate brand values and associations or not. Athletes' speech, therefore, helps form the brand—whether it comports or not with its usual messaging. This represents considerable power, as athletes can complicate and even contradict the preferred meanings of the leagues' brands.

These capabilities, it should be noted, are not open to all athletes in the same way and to the same degree. First, different leagues have different brands, some of which are more tolerant of certain speech. For example, the NWSL and WNBA have commonly allowed more progressive political expression than leagues like the NFL and NBA. Both leagues have allowed and even supported their athletes' fights against racism, homophobia, transphobia, and sexism. Second, each player is not afforded the same status to speak freely. Some players enjoy more celebrity status and are more visible than others—and therefore have more of a platform. For example, LeBron James has more power in the NBA than a bench player or someone in the league's minor league (the G League). The player's celebrity status doesn't need to be based on athletic performance, because the brands are built both inside and outside the competition. Athletes could have more power because their fame is based on their behavior outside of the competition; for example, Billy "White Shoes" Johnson and Ickey Woods were known for their touchdown celebrations, and Lamar Odom and Kris Humphries were famous for dating Kardashians. Furthermore, some athletes benefit from a mixture of competitive success and other considerations. Russell Wilson is a Super Bowl-winning quarterback married to R&B singer, Ciara, for instance. Shaquille O'Neal won multiple championships while starring in films and releasing rap albums. Celebrity athletes' visibility makes them more valuable to the leagues than less famous players, which sometimes, lessens the possibility that they will be punished or silenced.

We've already seen how leagues attempt to avoid certain constructions of Blackness in their brands, but certain forms of anti-racist activism are particularly in tension with the brands of the leagues. As we've seen, leagues attempt to brand themselves as being pure, apolitical, and meritocratic forms of entertainment. Calling out racism and white supremacy violates the notion of American meritocracy and therefore seems like a political intrusion into a pure sporting realm. That, of course, isn't to say that sports aren't rife with political meanings (Chapter 2) but that anti-racist messages are at odds with what is usually being communicated. There's a long history of athletes using their fame to speak out against racism and white supremacy, such as John Carlos, Tommie Smith, Muhammad Ali, Kareem Abdul-Jabbar, Bill Russell, and Mahmoud Abdul-Rauf. More recently, attention has migrated to issues of social justice that were popularized due to Black Lives Matter (BLM). Although BLM started after the 2012 killing of Trayvon Martin, "athlete support of BLM began garnering sustained national media attention in 2016" (Johnson, 2021, p. 119). Many athletes picked up activist actions that mirrored BLM's messages. These actions infused anti-racist messages into the leagues' brands before, during, and after games (Figure 3.1). For example, in 2014, LeBron James and

64 Live and Real Athlete Expression

FIGURE 3.1 During Fox Sports' post-game coverage of a Cleveland Cavaliers game, LeBron James is asked about his wearing an "I Can't Breathe" shirt during warmups to raise awareness of Eric Garner's killing at the hands of the New York Police.

other prominent basketball players wore "I Can't Breathe" shirts during their warmups in reference to the 2014 killing of Eric Garner by police and, in 2016, Colin Kaepernick knelt on the sidelines during the national anthem to protest social injustice.

Both actions infused anti-racist messages into the NBA's and NFL's brands. Players knew that performances of the national anthem and warmups were covered as part of the games. That's not to say either are always reported on or broadcasted, but when they are viewed as noteworthy, they become part of the coverage. As a result, both James and Kaepernick became topics of discussion: what they did; why they did it; and what it meant for the leagues, teams, and games (Lopez, 2020, pp. 73–74). Just as one might tune into a live broadcast or read a recap of game to see what happened during the competition, one might also want to see what James or Kaepernick did and how their teammates, the opposing team, and fans reacted. In this way, the liveness and realness of sports gets infused with activist messages. Game broadcasts and coverage involve other opportunities—pre- and post-game interviews, clothing, and shoes—to mix activism with the leagues' usual messages.

Since the genre of sports extends beyond competition, athletes can also infuse their activism into the brands of the leagues through social media. Social media give the impression that fans get to interact authentically with athletes, which enables athletes to brand themselves (Price et al., 2013, Schmittel & Sanderson, 2015). Their activities on social media, therefore, inform the public understanding of the players and forms narratives about them. These understandings are used and formed by leagues and media companies that wish to create the impression that sports involve real stories playing out live (Lopez, 2020, p. 74). The stories can be about sports, but social media posts can also focus on BLM, racism, and policing (Lopez, 2020, p. 74). These posts are fodder for discussion and analysis throughout the sports/media complex. Therefore, narratives about players are understood in the context of their online activism.

Highly publicized actions and philanthropy are also similarly represented throughout the sports/media complex. For example, LeBron James visibly fights for racial justice through his I Promise School and regular stances against policing violence, which affects the public understanding of who he is as a person. That isn't to say these are the only meanings he is associated with; it is common to hear about James's career's longevity, whether he's better than Michael Jordan, or even his business dealings and financial success. However, his activism, infused with on- and off-court meanings, still shapes a picture of who he is. Since the NBA and its partners are built on the expectation that athletes are represented as they really are, James's activism becomes part of the NBA.

Brand-building is a dynamic process that is always under construction and disputation. Activist athletes' anti-racist messages, as we've seen, conflict with basic tenants of the brands of the NBA and NFL, like their notion of apolitical meritocracy and pure competition. Due to the actions of athletes like James and Kaepernick, the usually dominant meanings in sports become contested, turning the leagues into spaces in which contradictory discourses jostle for visibility. Athletes gain significant power partially due to their fame but also from the leagues' commitment to liveness and realness. If players were portrayed merely as mindless robots who played their sport, there would be fewer opportunities for activists to infuse their messages into the leagues' brands. Instead, leagues benefit from humanizing players and creating narratives that seem real and that play out live. The result is that players' actions become part of the leagues, regardless of whether they align with the brand or not.

That said, athlete and brand messaging aren't always at odds. Take, for example, Michael Jordan. His brand involved remaining apolitical and representative of the meritocratic principle that hard work pays off (Andrews, 1996). These associations made him the perfect representative for the NBA and companies like McDonalds, Nike, and Gatorade. Other examples include cases mentioned earlier, such as when leagues adopt more progressive stances that fit with their players'. Both the WNBA and NWSL have been dedicated to anti-racism, anti-sexism, and anti-homophobia, which comports with many of their athletes' stances. This isn't to suggest that the leagues existed with these values first and then the athletes found space within those values to express themselves. Rather, the negotiation of branding made it possible for the leagues and athletes to collaboratively shape the meanings associated with both.

The Co-opting of Activism

The negotiations of meanings between the WNBA and the NWSL and their players foreground yet another form of league power: co-optation. By adopting the values and associations of the players, leagues can reshape them to suit their own purposes. Although the WNBA and NWSL mirror the messages of many of their outspoken players, not every league does so. Instead, leagues like the NBA and the NFL co-opt the messages of activist athletes to shift them closer to the leagues' pre-established values. The degree to which the leagues do so depends on the players' actions, the political context, and the particularities of the brands.

In response to athletes' interest in amplifying messages of racial equality and social justice, the NFL and NBA started media campaigns in 2018; the NFL released *Let's Listen Together* and NBA began *Voices*. Due to the explicitness of athletes' discussion of policing and racism, both leagues broke from their usual silence about racial inequity. These campaigns represented more than the athletes using their voice and popularity to imbue messages within the leagues' brands. They were a direct response to athletes pressuring the leagues to take a more ardent stance on the issue of race and social justice. These campaigns perform two important functions for the leagues. First, they alleviate the strain on the brand; rather than have the players and the leagues at odds espousing different messages, the campaigns offer an opportunity to appear unified. The desired message is that both the leagues and the players have come together over social justice and are now explicitly anti-racist. Such a shift brings a second benefit of marking the leagues as progressive in a way that is marketable. Like Sarah Banet-Weiser's (2013) discussion of how "new school" politics becomes commodified in children's television, the leagues can sell themselves with nods to liberal politics.

The campaigns give leagues more control over messages about racism and policing, as well as over the picture painted of their athletes. Like the other campaigns mentioned earlier, *Let's Listen Together* and *Voices* construct a supposedly wholesome view of the athletes by conforming athlete activism into messages in agreement with the leagues' usual values and associations. This commonly involves smoothing over activist messages that conflict with the brand. Take, for example, the tension between sports as an apolitical reflection of US meritocracy and the idea, raised by player activists, that Black communities are unjustly policed. If the NFL and NBA take on the latter, they must do so in ways that don't contradict the former. For this reason, the campaigns often downplay the structural and institutional reasons for the disproportional harm done to Black people by police. Instead of structural change, the leagues suggest the problem with policing comes down to a lack of interpersonal communication. This can be seen even in the titles—*Voices* and *Let's Listen Together*—which emphasize communicating. Furthermore, the leagues have focused on improving communication between the police and those policed by holding events intended to increase dialogue.

FIGURE 3.2   NBA stars meet with "local youth, law enforcement, and community leaders for a facilitated discussion about identity, inclusivity, allyship, equity, community safety, and strategies for building a stronger, safer and more inclusive Charlotte."

They arranged public panels in which community members, athletes, and police engage in public discussion (Figure 3.2). The message is clear: the problem with policing isn't the racism of the institution, but it is that there isn't enough conversation between the police and those policed. Such a framing implies that that the problems with policing fall partly on community members. Some parts of the campaigns go even further by suggesting that the problem is that the community doesn't understand the police. These aspects of the campaigns involve videos of players joining police patrols on "ride alongs." The suggestion is that policing would improve only if community members understand the police, their jobs, and their routines. This framing of policing problems and solutions not only shifts the focus from their institutional nature but also shifts the burden for change from the police to those policed.

Obviously, this is a change from original BLM activism, which was intended to remake or abolish the police by holding them accountable for the injustices they've perpetrated. The athlete activists weren't trying to start a dialogue and weren't pontificating about the everyday difficulty of policing—they were trying to effect anti-racist institutional change. The campaigns co-opted their efforts, and in the process erased the boldness of their politics. Leagues also shifted the topic away from policing entirely. Concerns about social justice were outright eliminated and replaced with player efforts involving events that aligned with the brands' usual associations—mentoring, peace, history, and diversity—rather than racism and policing. Therefore, the leagues' connection to apolitical meritocracy can remain.

Another benefit of campaigns is that they are malleable, and therefore can respond to new events. In 2020, during the COVID-19 pandemic, there was yet another round of high-profile killings by the police: George Floyd, Breonna Taylor, and Jacob Blake. Their deaths sparked protests around the globe, including within the sporting world. Player activism became more widespread; kneeling during the anthem became commonplace and there was a strike in the NBA after the killing of Jacob Blake. The slayings also caught the attention of the leagues, who accepted BLM shirts and signage and the players again pressured teams and leagues to make official statements. The league shifted their response; the NFL's *Let's Listen Together* became *Inspire Change*, while *NBA Voices* took on social justice more explicitly. While most of the themes mentioned earlier were still present—there was a focus on community-building and the history of civil rights and social justice—the framings shifted to match the contemporary moment.

Before 2020, the NFL was extremely reticent to talk about actual cases of police injustice. This changed during the pandemic. The NFL's *Inspire Change* started a "Say Their Stories" Campaign that highlighted people who had been killed by the police. Of the 87 memorials, there were two varieties: videos narrated by players, and stills with text written by relatives or loved ones. There was, however, almost no mention of institutionalized racism or commentary about what needs to change to avoid future murders. While the leagues actually did, as protesters requested, say their names, it came at the expense of a direct political conversation about systemic racism. *NBA Voices* was willing to engage with more details about institutional inequality. They'd mention "racial injustice" or "Black Lives Matter," and post about housing, voting, and educational inequalities. However, there was a lack of substantial discussion about abolishing or defunding the police and few concrete solutions to problems of policing brought up by the players. Both leagues also repurposed the pre-pandemic protests they ignored or silenced. The NFL, for example, in its Inspire Change Super Bowl ad, hypocritically used images of players kneeling on the field to announce its commitment of $250 million "to help end systemic racism." These campaigns "play politics without doing it [and] delight in political speech without the work involved in organizing and forming coalitions" (Johnson, 2021, p. 135).

So, league-created campaigns started to address certain components of athlete activist messaging during the summer of 2020. They regularly mentioned concepts and phrases that were usually avoided, like BLM, racial injustice, and systemic racism. However, the leagues still regularly avoided certain core components of the BLM movement and the leagues' own roles in silencing the fight for racial justice. With regard to BLM, while there was more frequent mentioning of police and institutional racism, there still was reticence to connect the two. The concept that the institution of policing is racist and therefore needs to be defunded or abolished was missing. In other words, the notion of institutionalized racism became hazy, abstracted from details about which institutions were racist and how specifically they harmed people of color. There was also no discussion of concrete ways to change the institution by being defunded or abolished. The end goals of player and BLM activism—changing institutions to save peoples' lives—were lost in the leagues' co-opting of activist symbols.

Finally, while a lot of the activism has focused on policing, it is also worth noting that the leagues ended up erasing their own histories of racism. The NFL and NBA—like MLB and Jackie Robinson—celebrate the players who broke the color barrier. They foreground them as brave heroes who overcame racism, without noting which institution prohibited the athletes from playing. All the specifics about who is responsible for harm and how it occurred were lacking. There's no sense that the leagues were at fault, or need to apologize or change. Instead, they framed themselves in a relatively positive light as the institutions that let pioneering Black players into their games. In these ways, leagues portray themselves as progressive leaders rather than racist perpetrators.

Co-opting athlete expression into brand-friendly labor policy and media campaigns needs time to develop and implement. Even reactionary strategies like dress codes and the 2020 BLM media campaigns are drafted and implemented in an organized, top–down manner. Additionally, since brands communicate values to and through its network, other entities can act in agreement, even without prior planning. An instance of such tacit agreement happened in 2017, when President Trump called any player who knelt during an NFL game a "son of a bitch" who deserved to be fired. In the following week's games, many players knelt, stood with a fist raised, or avoided the sideline during the national anthem. Powerful images of entire teams participating in these actions circulated, some of whom were joined by coaches and team owners. These widespread images created a problem for the NFL's brand, which remained connected to pro-militaristic expressions of patriotism during the national anthem in which any other political expressions are viewed as foreign and worthy of censure. Without recourse to previously established labor policies and media campaigns, the NFL resorted to an *ad hoc* way of protecting its brand from athlete activism: franchise owners, team managers, and coaches simply translated athlete activism through public statements and social media as conforming to the brand's usual values. In the process, they minimized the political messages about racial justice, policing, and protesting Trump (Lopez, 2021). There was a "regular tendency by league administrators to protect the NFL's usual associations and values" while "still giving the appearance of support of the players" (Lopez, 2021, p. 10).

Therefore, the brands of the leagues have significant power with respect to inhibiting athlete activism. Not only can leagues use organized and formal methods like media campaigns to morph the athletes' political messages into a form more consistent with their brands, the brands themselves also arrange a fairly uniform and yet more *ad hoc* response from league administrators. Both coping mechanisms work on two fronts: they superficially shift the leagues' usual meanings and associations, and reshape the meanings of athlete expression to be more aligned with the brand. For the former, because the athletes could import activism into the brands, the leagues need to re-create the feeling of consistency. That is, if they won't or can't try to silence athletes, they need to respond by further shifting themselves toward the athletes' messages. Such a shift was seen when the campaigns mentioned policing and BLM, or when team administrators knelt on the field with the athletes in response to Trump. However, because the brands have been successful, the leagues won't commit to a branding overhaul. To maintain the appearance of being consistent with athlete expression, the leagues simply co-opt them to match their usual values and associations.

Conclusion: The Live and Real Power Play

There is a power struggle between the leagues and their players that unfolds through branding. The leagues brand themselves has having a live and real product in which the actual personalities of the players are on display, both inside and outside the competition. Such framings grant athletes leeway to express themselves throughout the sports/media complex and inject messages that could be foreign or even contradictory to those of the leagues. In response, leagues can enact strategies that attempt to shape athlete speech through league policies, media campaigns, and more *ad hoc* methods like commentary by league administrators. However, as long as leagues brand themselves as representing players in a live and real fashion, branding conflict will endure. Players will retain the ability to insert messages of their choosing into the brand, and leagues will try to constrain and reinterpret their messages.

The athletes' brand-shaping power also does not come without potential consequences. Athletes could choose to speak in ways that will get them fined because they feel their message is more important than the money lost. However, not every player will make this decision and not all can afford the reduced pay. Furthermore, given the web of interrelated branded values, a violation of the leagues' brands could result in a violation of their sponsors' brands. In other words, athletes could lose valuable sponsorship deals. Because of these threats, no athlete is entirely free to speak out. Instead, this chapter has described the conditions in which their expressions can compete with league messaging. And, despite these incredible pressures, some athletes have cultivated substantial power to alter the leagues' brands.

Before the end of this chapter, it is necessary to widen the scope of our discussion. There are, after all, other expressions besides activism against racism, and other people involved in league brand-building besides athletes. I chose anti-racist activism to discuss because it offers a vibrant example of the power struggle between classic league values and athlete politics. There are, however, other values that leagues protect using policy. Leagues will, for example, fine their players if they find that they used a racist or homophobic slur. These cases, however, need to be contextualized within the backdrop of the leagues' history of institutionalized anti-Blackness (and homophobia). Just as with the other policies surveyed earlier, these sanctioning efforts are intended to discourage players from acting in ways that would harm the brand. Slurs explicitly undercut the notion that sports are an apolitical meritocracy by challenging the idea that they are free of discrimination and that all that matters is competitive performance. While the anti-slur policies could be thought of as being anti-racist or anti-homophobic, they are inexorably part of a system that polices its largely Black labor force and obscures institutionalized racism.

Given the way that sports organizations are set up, players are not the only people responsible for building the brand. They certainly are the center, but the expression of coaches and team managers are also surveilled and can be punished. Fines against coaches are commonly levied for criticizing referees. While players can be fined for this as well, sometimes coaches take it upon themselves to speak critically about the way a game was called to try to change refereeing practices in future games. However, whether speaking strategically or out of frustration, coaches can be fined for negative commentary about the way the sport is refereed. These fines operate similarly to the anti-gambling policies discussed in Chapter 1 and therefore are similarly used to protect the expectation of live and real competition. In order for competition to seem real, it must be presented as honest; the idea that gamblers might "fix" the game undercuts an honest image. The same goes for refereeing; the idea that referees might get calls wrong or be biased disrupts the supposedly pure competition. Such ideas advance the notion that outside elements could inform what happens in the game and therefore critiques of how games are called can be tolerated only up to a point. If referees are making mistakes, then the competition is no longer a pure meritocracy.

Finally, the leagues' brands are also composed of the understandings and actions of fans and audiences. Chapter 4 will focus on how fans construct and expect the genre of live and real competition. For the purposes of this chapter, however, it is worth considering how fans and activists can use the liveness of sports to communicate in ways similar to athletes. Activists can protest before the competition, which is what Indigenous name change activists did to attempt to sway opinion on the name of the NFL's Washington-based team (Lopez & Lopez, 2017). These activists helped create and shape a story that was covered throughout sports media about the team's name, which was as a slur. Being at games was a major part of their communication strategy (Lopez & Lopez, 2017), which helped to spread their message within the NFL football community. Protests outside of the competition, however, have the drawback of depending on outside coverage.

While activists can make their own media campaigns, their ability to spread messages to a wider (sports) audience is often contingent on their story getting taken up by powerful sports media companies. This is why some activists choose to make use of the liveness and realness of sports competitions by interrupting them. For one example, animal rights activist Alicia Santurio attempted to protest "the mass killing of chickens at Glen Taylor's factory farm by gluing herself onto the floor during a 2022 playoff game between Taylor's Minnesota Timberwolves and the Los Angeles Clippers" (Bartov, 2022). Even though the television announcers struggled to understand her actions, they were caught live on television and shared widely through social media, where Santurio was dubbed #GlueGirl (Bartov, 2022). A second example occurred later in the year when a climate-change activist interrupted a French Open men's semifinal by tying herself to the net while wearing a shirt that read "we have 1028 days left" (Gonzalez, 2022). Despite the fact that live broadcasters can use the broadcast's delay and can cut away from the activism, protesters can use the element of surprise to get their message through. Furthermore, as we saw in the first chapter, the notion of liveness and realness is supported by social media. Even when broadcasters manage to avoid showing the activism, it is still caught on phone cameras and spread online. In this way, activists' messages end up being echoed throughout the discussion of the competition itself.

Protests that occur during games, therefore, function similarly whether they are conducted by athletes or non-athletes. Spectators are a major component of how leagues mark themselves as being live and real. Of course, minus celebrity fans like Jack Nicholson and Drake, fans are usually covered as a whole and not as individuals. Still, non-athlete activists can interrupt the normal rhythms of the game to garner attention, just as athletes do. Furthermore, their actions—like athlete activists—fold their political messages into the brands of the leagues. Both forms of protest depend on the leagues' commitment to live and real competition being a part of their entertainment brand. Without this generic convention being constructed the way that it is, activists wouldn't have the power to communicate through the brand of the leagues. That is, the structures and meanings of live and real competition surveyed in Chapters 1 and 2 form the context and basis from which sports activism derives its power.

Bibliography

Andrews, D. (1996). The Fact(s) of Michael Jordan's Blackness: An Excavation in Four Parts. *Sociology of Sport Journal*, 13(2), 125–158.

Banet-Weiser, S. (2013). What's Your Flava?: Race and Postfeminism in Media Culture. In L. Ouellette (Ed.), *The Media Studies Reader* (pp. 379–393). Routledge.

Bartov, S. (2022). "Glue Girl" Protests Timberwolves Owner by Sticking Self to NBA Court. *Newsweek.com*. www.newsweek.com/glue-girl-protests-timerwolves-owner-sticking-self-nba-court-minnesota-1697772

Cunningham, P. (2009). "Please Don't Fine Me Again!!!!!": Black Athletic Defiance in the NBA and NFL. *Journal of Sport and Social Issues*, 33(1), 39–58.

Edwards, H. (2017). *The Revolt of the Black Athlete*. University of Illinois Press.

Gonzalez, I. (2022). LOOK: Protestor Ties Herself to Net During 2022 French Open Men's Semifinal Between Casper Ruud, Marin Cilic. *CBS Sports.com*. www.cbssports.com/tennis/news/look-protestor-ties-herself-to-net-during-2022-french-open-mens-semifinal-between-casper-ruud-marin-cilic/

Grainger, A., Newman, J. & Andrews, D. (2006). Sport, the Media, and the Construction of Race. In A. Raney & J. Bryant (Eds.), *Handbook of Sports and Media* (pp. 447–468). Routledge.

Gray, J. (2010). *Show Sold Separately: Promos, Spoilers, and Other Media Paratexts*. New York University Press.

Johnson, V. (2021). *Sports TV*. Routledge.

Lopez, J. (2020). Branding Athlete Activism. In L. Lopez (Ed.), *Race and Media: Critical Approaches* (pp. 67–78). New York University Press.

Lopez, J. (2021). Rewriting Activism: The NFL Takes a Knee. *Critical Studies in Media Communication*, 38(2), 183–196.

Lopez, L. & Lopez, J. (2017). Deploying Oppositional Fandoms: Activists' Use of Sports Fandom in the Redskins Controversy. In J. Gray, C. Sandvoss, & C. Harrington (Eds.), *Fandom: Identities and Communities in a Mediated World* (pp. 315–332). New York University Press.

Lury, C. (2004). *Brands: The Logos of the Global Economy*. Routledge.

Oriard, M. (2003). *Brand NFL: Making & Selling America's Favorite Sport*. University of North Carolina Press.

Price, J., Farrington, N. & Hall, L. (2013). Changing the Game? The Impact of Twitter on Relationships Between Football Clubs, Supporters and the Sports Media. *Soccer & Society*, 14(4), 446–461.

Schmittel, A. & Sanderson, J. (2015). Talking about Trayvon in 140 Characters: Exploring NFL Players' Tweets About the George Zimmerman Verdict. *Journal of Sports and Social Issues*, 39(4), 332–345.

4
FANS OF LIVE AND REAL COMPETITION

Two strangers pass on the street, note each other's shirt, and nod their heads in recognition. Or, they are at a bar and strike up a conversation about home and family. Or, they recite history and statistics to pass time at work. Or, they suspiciously eye each other at a mutual friend's social event. The motivating factor in all of these vignettes could be sports fandom. Because sports are part of popular culture, they offer salient meanings for fans to operate within; they help people make sense of the world and each other. A fan of the Los Angeles Dodgers is probably from or has a connection to Southern California. A fan of the Las Vegas Aces is likely to know they won their first Championship in 2022. The chances that a fan of Megan Rapinoe enjoys her bold play and confidence on the pitch are high.

Sports fandom, like all fandoms, involves personal identification. Fandom becomes a way of stating one's identity, values, and engagement with the world. This performance of self through sports can be both consumptive (Sandvoss, 2003) and participatory (Halverson & Halverson, 2008) in nature. Indeed, how fans say who they are through fandom is incredibly diverse and involves much more than just sitting down to watch a game—and might not even involve that in the first place. Fans can wear, read, study, eat, drink, and play their fandom. The purpose of this chapter, therefore, is to see how the diversity of fan self-expression engages with the genre of sports.

We've seen that sports media industries encourage viewing sports in a certain way, yet fans can accept or reject these constructions. The industries respond to fans, creating a loop in which the genre is constructed through their interplay with fans. In this chapter, we will explore how fans construct the idea that sports

DOI: 10.4324/9781003164272-5

media involve live and real competition. This is not, however, to take up a deterministic position in which fan engagement is constrained by the sports media industries. Instead, fandom is a powerful force that, in conjunction with sports media industries, creates the generic expectations of sports media. In other words, the context of fan identification involves the interplay of "structure (norms and limits) versus agency (individual capacity to make choices)" (Georgiou, 2017, p. 95). Fans have choice, but it is also important to note how "inscriptions of identity are reproduced through the repetition of certain symbols, not least through media representation" (Georgiou, 2017, p. 97). The larger context of fandom matters.

As an entertainment product, some of the symbols' contexts come from how sports are branded (Chapter 1). The self-performance of sports fandom, therefore, happens through fans engaging with branding. Sarah Banet-Weiser notes that "[b]rands become the setting around which individuals weave their own stories, where individuals position themselves as the central character in the narrative of the brand: 'I'm an iPhone,' or 'I drink Coke'" (2017, p. 26). Identification can be particularly strong in sports. It is telling that sports fans identify with their object of fandom uniquely using the words "we" and "us." For team sports in particular, a fan might talk about the fact that "we need a win" or "this has been a tough stretch for us." These are linguistic markers of how sports fandom powerfully informs an individual's self-expression and self-understanding. Such deep self-identification is not itself unique; fans of, say, Disney organize their lives to make trips to theme parks, their daily schedule around engaging with media, and their budget to support buying merchandise. However, since we've seen that sports have their own particular generic markers, it is important to consider how fan identification interacts with them. In this chapter, we will explore how fans support and construct the notion that sports are live and real competition.

To help organize the study of fans, the chapter will be organized according to Abercrombie and Longhursts's (1998) taxonomy of audiences, as described by Hills (2017, p. 18) in the following:

1. Simple: being co-present at events
2. Mass: watching in ways "emblematic of large-scale TV audiences watching [synchronously] according to 'linear' scheduling models"
3. Diffused: engaging through ways that are nonlinear and on-demand like social media and blogs

Given the scope of this book on sports media, most of this chapter's focus will be on Mass and Diffused ways of engaging with sports. How do Mass and Diffused fans, along with the rest of the sports/media complex, form the genre of sports?

Conceptualizing Fans of Live and Real Competition

Before focusing on fan expression through media in the remainder of the chapter, this section will explicate a general conception of fandom from which to start the analysis. Because of the focus on live and real competition, let's begin with a common conception of fans at a sports event. In this context, one might picture a particular image: people loudly and enthusiastically cheering in the stands during a game. This is the Simple conception of fandom. While some of the details might change—Are they holding signs? Are they wearing jerseys? Have they painted their faces and bodies? Are they drinking beer?—such images are a common way fans are portrayed. These pictures' familiarity is partially due to the expectation of live and real competition; sports fans go to real competitions and watch them play out live.

While Simple and enthusiastic fandom must be accounted for, it is too narrow to base a full notion of fandom. First, contemporary versions of Simple participation have been shaped by the Mass and Diffused experiences. PA announcers, hype music, scoreboards with stats, video montages, and advertisements all show how elements of mediated engagement with sports have spread into the in-person experience. Therefore, the ways fans participate in the genre of sports media can, in some instances, be read back into Simple engagements. That is, though Simple fandom might be a good basis from which to start an analysis, it is not all-encompassing. Second, fan engagement can be extremely diverse and go beyond the notion of the enthusiastic fan. An account of sports fandom must reckon with its heterogeneity.

Although the notion of fans rooting at a game is too narrow to base a full description of sports fandom on, it does highlight that fandom is an activity. Fans at games can cheer, brandish signs, and eat and drink. Note, these don't have to be particularly vigorous; even paying for tickets, driving and parking at a venue, and sitting through a game is enough to be considered an activity. That is, even fan expression that might at first glance seem passive still involves the fan doing things. What, therefore, is the sports-specific unifier of these activities?

One might say it is the affective connection to sports that is unique. When fans attend games, they commonly yell, cheer, and boo (Figure 4.1). These actions are connected to emotions, both negative and positive. This is important, as feelings—and even strong feelings—can be a regular component of fandom (Jhally, 1989, p. 73). Take typical expressions of fan emotion: nervously biting one's nails during a close game, hugging fellow fans after a big win, crying or booing after a loss. However, not every fan expression needs to be so charged. Fans can be mildly interested or even bored. Furthermore, emotions can fluctuate over the course of a lifetime, season, or even game. For example, consider fans who tend to engage more when their team is winning, plays a certain style of game, uses a certain strategy, or has a popular player.

FIGURE 4.1 The assumed picture of sports fans: those enthusiastically cheering on their team in the stands of the competition. The MLB's video following the Dodger fan club, Pantone 294, claims that it is "the best Dodger experience ever."

A corollary of shifting fan engagement is that there is little theoretical reason to seek a "true" fandom. Take, for example, much derided fans like fair-weather fans (those who are interested in their team only when successful) or bandwagon fans (those who start rooting for a team when they become successful). Regardless, no one is born into a fandom and everyone's interest waxes and wanes for their own reasons. But just because there is no theoretical grounding to justify the differentiation between the validity of emotions for "real" versus "bandwagon" fans, it doesn't follow that fans don't perceive such a differentiation. While heightened emotion cannot be the cornerstone of fandom, a description of sports fandom must reckon with it since it does indeed occur.

Strong emotions are part of fandom because people use their fandom to express who they are. In other words, fandom is a form of self-expression that is meant to communicate who a person is. In this way, fandom is part of identity and self-reflection (Sandvoss, 2003). Sports fan identity expression can be as varied as the many broad ways one can express one's identity (Kerwin & Hoeber, 2022). One's values, roles, and community can all get wrapped up in what it means to be fan (Sandvoss, 2003). Sports fandom is a way of saying who you are. The community aspect is particularly salient in sports. A shared group can be organized based on a particular time and place, as when fans assemble to watch a game. It can also be constructed in a more abstract sense, when fans identify with the team and each other outside of the circumstances of any particular game. Fan group identity can be formed around family, friends, and location. For example, identifying as a Los Angeles Dodger fan can be meant to reflect one's friends from LA, a multigenerational familial commitment to the team, and one's connection to Southern California. It can also create community around valuing being hard-working, blue collar, underdogs, and so on.

In this way, sports can create the perception that there is a community of "us." And, a construction of an "us" also involves a construction of a "them" (Crawford, 2004, p. 55). Rivalries are a salient opportunity for in- and out-group building, as rivals regularly compete against each other and, therefore, are dependable opportunities to build groups. Due to geographical proximity and MLB scheduling in which San Francisco Giants play the Dodgers, the relationship between the two teams is a fairly stable way to organize insiders and outsiders. However, even the regular opposition of competitors in each game throughout a season delineates who the "we" and "they" are. All of the Dodgers's 162 regular season games are opportunities to root against for the opposition as outsiders.

Fans can also create an image of themselves by contrasting themselves with fans with same rooting interests. In other words, lines can be drawn between "real" fans and "fake" fans. Distinctions are drawn, as noted earlier, between "true" fans and bandwagon or fair-weather fans. But, furthermore, distinctions between insiders and outsiders are often informed by culturally salient ideologies and make use of categories like race, gender, class, and sexuality. For example, a fan of the Chelsea soccer team who holds cosmopolitan values might be inclined to see the team and its fans as inclusive, while a racist fan could see the same fan/team unity as good because it is the "white club" (Sandvoss, 2003, p. 37). Because these are cultural constructs, they can shift over time, but they do represent fairly stable ways for fans to construct and reflect upon themselves. Cosmopolitan Chelsea fans create a notion of who they are as people and a group, and those who don't share their values—even if they root for Chelsea—are not "true" Chelsea fans. Racist fans can use the same logic.

Although fan identities are in conversation with social constructs, it doesn't follow that fans must always uphold messages found commonly in sports. Certainly, hegemonic messages are extremely available for fans, but they can be resisted and transgressed. For example, fans can express disfavor with their teams' competitive performance, as when in-stadia fans of the NFL's Cleveland Browns put bags on their heads to demonstrate their embarrassment with their connection to the team. Cutting against the expectation that fans always support their teams, these fans demonstrated their dissatisfaction. Fans can also transgress more culturally inscribed messages. In earlier chapters we saw that sports can be a hostile place for women, but fan-activists can organize for gender equity (Dimitrov, 2008). Even cases of resistance, however, involve using sports to construct one's identity—one person might value winning or effort, while another could value gender equality.

The idea that fans identify with their object of fandom is not unique to sports. Fans of a media franchise like *Star Wars* or a musician like Lizzo could read their values, histories, and communities onto their favorite sci-fi franchise or singer. However, there are novelties of sports fandom that are heightened through being connected to sports, many of which are informed by the generic conventions of sports. To start, we saw previously that sports fandoms being organized around regular competition allow for robust opportunities for creating a notion of oneself through juxtaposition. "Oppositional fandom" is the result of any game or match in which fans have contradictory rooting interests (Lopez & Lopez, 2017). If I, as a Portland Thorns fan, am rooting for my team when they play the Houston Dash, then I am also rooting against the Dash and their fans. Some fan oppositions, however, go even deeper than this because they are long-standing and inscribed with more cultural meaning. Because sports often involve rivalries, they are notable opportunities for expressions of anti-fandom (Theodoropoulou, 2007). Although opposition and defining oneself through juxtaposition happens in other contexts (*Star Wars* fans versus *Star Trek* fans, fans of The Notorious B.I.G. vs. fans of Tupac Shakur), sports' competition offers regular opportunities and robust meanings for identity construction through juxtaposition.

The liveness and realness of sports competition informs the powerful emotive connections to sports. Similarly strong emotions can be found in Asian American audiences at showings of *Crazy Rich Asians* (Lopez, 2021a) and from Black audiences at *Black Panther* (Wallace, 2018), for example. However, the notions of liveness, realness, and competition can augment or increase the opportunities for intense emotional connections. First, fan identity gets attached to something that has been manufactured as real. This means there are "real" stakes for one's construction of self through sports. Furthermore, because sports are competitions, there are winners and losers. It follows that it isn't only the participants in the games who are victorious or defeated, it is also the fans themselves—their values, communities, histories. Finally, because sports are live, fans can't know which side they are on until the event happens; their personal success or losing happens in the moment. During games, sports fans watch themselves win or lose live, which understandably can be a situation fraught with emotion.

Sports-specific opportunities help fans express their selves through fandom. Sports fandom involves consumption: watching games, reading news, buying merchandise, and even eating and drinking (Billings, 2014; Crawford, 2004; Sandvoss, 2003). Fans of the *Harry Potter* franchise might do all these things by watching the movies, reading the books, buying a wand, and drinking butterbeer. However, fandom is more than consumption—it is the specifics of how the consumption happens. For this reason, sports fandom can be thought of as a particular performance (Crawford, 2004, p. 122). To understand the novelties of sports, attention must be paid to both what is consumed and how it is consumed.

Given that Simple engagements with sports are situated as the center of sports fandom, the particularities of consumption can be located in fan expression in stadia. Such expressions involve being sensitive to how fans behave, and how that behavior is encouraged within the sporting environment. It is important to reiterate that the live event is not the only or central expression of fandom. However, due to the centrality of live and real competition, it is often *assumed* to be the prototypical way of engaging with sports. So, even though some fans of sports might rarely watch a live game in person, the genre of sports is built upon foregrounding live and real competition, which then spreads throughout the sports media universe. The genre's perceived centrality results in stadia being compared to religious or educational sites, and even being considered "home" (Crawford, 2004, p. 66).

Stadia are designed to reflect the consumptive nature of sports fandom. Sports venues have been "mallified"—they now resemble malls and fans shop there accordingly (Guilianotti, 1999, p. 83). Mallification places an importance not just on merchandise but also on food and drink (Parry & Richards, 2022). Furthermore, arenas are more than sites for the commodification of fandom, they are themselves commodities used for fannish purposes. In a crowded market for live entertainment and leisure experiences, sports venues must separate themselves from the other options (Crawford, 2004, p. 82). Such a distinction involves shaping the entertainment product itself to be as engaging as possible by adding elements that surround the game like cheerleaders, music, announcers, and video displays. As with the genre of sports, the commodification of live sports experiences involves more than just the competitive product. Sports venues, therefore, must offer an entertainment experience that differs from similar environments that depend on spectacle (Crawford, 2004, p. 82). The games, shopping, food and drink, halftime dance routines, pregame singing of the national anthem, mascots, and jumbotron-based entertainment like the "kiss cam" and quiz games, all mark the experience of being at a game as a unique act of consumption. Different sports and even teams market their games based on the novelty of these events. MLB offers a "first pitch" and MLB teams distinguish themselves based on experiential criteria: fans of the Los Angeles Dodgers can eat the Dodger Dog, the Milwaukee Brewers's fans cheer the racing sausages, and Chicago Cubs fans sing along to Harry Caray's rendition of *Take Me Out to the Ballgame*. Sports fandom's performative consumption is expressed throughout the live sports experience.

Simple audiences are often the default picture of the sports fan due to the expectation of live and real competition. Sports do indeed offer fans competition that plays out live, which isn't as available in other types of entertainment. However, we've seen earlier that fan behavior is so much more than cheering at a game; it involves self-identification and self-reflection expressed through performative consumption. In the rest of the section, we'll see how this basic conception of fandom can play out in Mass and Diffused audiences.

Mass Fandoms of Live and Real Competition

Liveness is a major selling point of broadcast of sports events (Chapter 1). Media industries regard the sport genre as valuable because it is considered "appointment viewing" for Mass audiences. Even events that aren't as big as the Super Bowl or March Madness still retain the allure of liveness. Broadcasts of live sporting events are used to attract audiences to streaming services, for example. ESPN+ leverages sports that are more niche to American audiences (like Italian Serie A soccer, the Rainbow Cup rugby tournament, and UFC fights) to coax fans to pay for the subscription service (Lopez, 2022). Furthermore, gaming companies like DraftKings offer streaming of German Bundesliga soccer and the Korean Baseball Association to drive gamers to their mobile applications. These contemporary cases reflect bidding wars for television broadcast rights for major sports. All these industrial narratives assume that sports fans value live and real competition.

When tied to the conception of fandom discussed earlier, it follows that fans esteem watching live and real Mass broadcasts because they are opportunities for self-expression that parallel those of a live event. This assumed connection comes from the considerations mentioned in the first two chapters; companies that offer live broadcasts of games communicate that they are offering an experience that's like being at the game. From how the games are advertised to how they are shot and commented upon, fans are told that the consumptive act of watching a game on television is like watching a game at a stadium. It is unsurprising, therefore, that the markers of fandom discussed earlier can be found even in fans watching the game at home: having heightened emotions, cheering, booing, wearing merchandise, eating certain food, drinking specific beverages, and congregating with friends and family. Live broadcasts—because of their industry-based tie to the live and real competitive event—offer an opportunity for similar fannish expressions.

However, mediated liveness is highly constructed and involves experiences that aren't found in actual live events (Chapters 1 and 2). Live commentary, views from around the stadium, regular close-up and slow motion replays, on-screen statistics, and commercials all have become part of the broadcast of live and real competition. These differences can allow broadcasters to shape the experience of fans by calling attention to narratives and aspects of the games. Therefore, mediated liveness also shapes the meanings that fans ascribe to their fandom. As stated earlier, this isn't to assume a deterministic picture in which fans must conform to the dominant readings from broadcasters. Instead, I argue that they are powerful conveyers of meanings that fandoms will be in conversation with. For example, a Los Angeles Dodger could be pitching a perfect game and some fans in Dodger Stadium might be aware of that fact. Broadcasters could highlight this potential milestone, contextualize it within Dodger and MLB history, and narrativize it through the pitcher's personal history. Fans watching that broadcast, therefore, have access to readings that connect to their fandom that are less available to the in-stadium fans; they can feel pride at historical Dodger pitching success or relate to the pitcher's story of hard work and perseverance.

Broadcasts are watched in spaces that associate different meanings and fan expressions with sports. For example, some establishments exhibited closed-circuit television broadcasts for an audience who would pay admission (Johnson, 2021, p. 146). The resulting atmosphere was akin to an in-stadia event in which a group of people watched a competitive event unfold. While closed-circuit television has waned as a medium for sport, watching broadcasts as a group in public has not. Fans now use spaces like bars to perform their fandom. In some cases, their performance involves importing norms from watching a game in one's "home" stadium; seating arrangements can replicate stands, food and drink usually found in the stadium might be consumed, and apparel is commonly worn (Kraszewski, 2008). All of these similarities perform notions of one's identity, community, and home (Kraszewski, 2008). However, not every aspect of public consumption of sports broadcasts needs to mirror the in-stadia experience. Some fans might prefer performing their fandom at a bar due to its differences from the live stadium. There are usually no entrance fees and food normally is cheaper, and behavior allowed at the bar might not be allowed at a stadium (Weed, 2007). However, some fans prefer off-site viewing as a way of feeling proximate to the game (Weed, 2007), which is a reminder that all fan engagement—including fan engagement in bars and stadia—are consumptive performances that demonstrate the centrality of live and real competition. Fans hold value in some notion of "being there" and use that construction, especially in groups, to perform and consume.

Of course, not all expressions of sports fandom need to involve groups depending on one's circumstances or preferences. Even what it means to watch an event with others can have extreme variability; watching from the stands, from the bar, or even at home along with the rest of the at-home broadcast audience could all represent an opportunity for fan performance of "being at" the game. Each mode of watching affords different expressions that import the notion of experiencing live sports into one's fandom—and therefore one's conception of self.

Diffused Fandoms of Live and Real Competition

Both the diversity of contexts in which sports are watched and the similarity in how those experiences reflect watching live and real competition are salient in digital engagements. Just as with Mass audiences, Diffused audiences use the affordances of different media and technology to perform their fandom and express their identity. The diversity of ways that fans consume sports digitally allows for a myriad of fan performances. Even in the heterogeneous digital realm, however, fan connection to live and real competition remains a central theme.

Accessibility and mobility are hallmarks of Diffused engagements. Although not everyone has the same access to digital media, their ability to democratize

Fans of Live and Real Competition   83

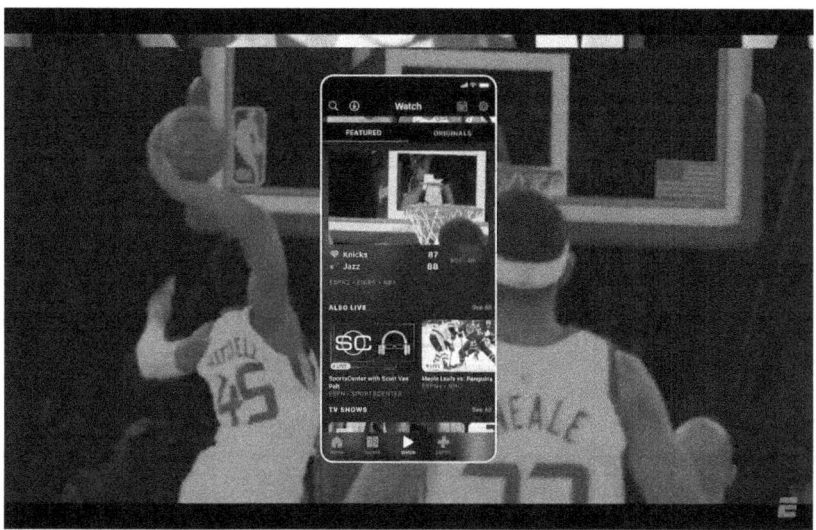

FIGURE 4.2   An ad for ESPN's mobile application, claiming that it offers diffused fans "One App, One Tap" for all their sports interests.

participation with sports media allows digital sports media to become a form of "mundane software" that "embeds [mediated experiences] more deeply in everyday practices" (Morris & Elkins, 2015, p. 62). Just as a Daily Fantasy Sports (DFS) mobile application like DraftKings can turn any space into a sports gaming space (Lopez, 2018), sports digital media allows for a mundane and everyday sports engagement that can happen in many places. As an act of performative consumption, fans can stream games on ESPN+, read social media for news, and play games on DraftKings to express their fandom. The folding of fan expression into everyday life only adds to the feeling of the realness of sports. When sports become intertwined with one's mundane everyday activities, fan expression becomes more cemented into how fans express themselves throughout the day, thereby making the expression seem like a major component of who the fans really are (Figure 4.2). So although the conception of sports fandom that comes to mind quickest might be the Simple version—attending a live game in-venue—Diffused engagement is also an extremely common and fitting expression of fandom of live and real competition.

Although accessibility and mobility are often shared by digital fan expression, it is also worth attending to how it might vary depending on the technology. Indeed, each form of media technology affords distinct fan expressions. The particularities of social media, for example, allow fans to self-express in ways that other forms of digital sports media (e.g., streaming and gaming) don't. In fact, social media offer unique opportunities for fans to express and strengthen their fandom (Kennedy et al., 2022). Many social media platforms like Twitter, Instagram, and Facebook involve the creation of a profile, which include the option to list one's interests, select a username, and display a photo (Coduto, 2022). Fans of a team like the WNBA's Las Vegas Aces could mention their fandom of the team, city, or a player like A'ja Wilson. They might also make "Aces" part of their profile name or select their logo for their profile picture. Social media allow users to post texts, pictures, and videos to their individual feeds, which are viewable by others (Coduto, 2022). Different platforms might have different emphases (Twitter and text, Instagram and photos, TikTok and video), but there is an increasing tendency for their convergence into a single platform. However, they all offer opportunities for identity construction through fandom; fans might post a written ode to a favorite player's performance, a photo of them wearing the jersey of their favorite team, or a video taken at the arena. Although each social media platform has different affordances, they all grant fans the opportunity to incorporate sports fandom into an online presentation of who they are.

These self-presentations are, as the name suggests, social in nature. Profiles and posts are constructed to be seen. While some users might restrict who can find them or see their posts, interaction is at the center of social media. Therefore, they are opportunities for the community-building often connected to sports fandom. By following and being followed by others, fans can create networks to engage with those with similar interests and expressions of those interests. Interaction is enabled through commenting functions, thereby allowing exchanges beyond the simple reading of posts. To be able to engage with other users in this way, social media must be searchable, and a powerful tool for doing so is the hashtag (Coduto, 2022, p. 280). In preparation for a Las Vegas Aces and Seattle Storm WNBA playoff game, an Aces fan might search Twitter for relevant hashtags like #LasVegasAces, #WNBAPlayoffs, or #StormBasketball. By using hashtags, commenting on others' posts, and creating groups, fans can grow community around their fandom on social media.

The self-presentation of fandom on social media allows the markers of Simple and Mass fandom—personal associations, values, and community—to be expressed. On social media, however, we see fan identification powerfully associated with the genre of sports. Due to their affordances, social media are apt sites for the expression of the generic associations of liveness and realness (Chapter 1). Social media's immediacy allows synchronous conversations with live events and the rapid distribution of news stories. Fan expression on social media, therefore, is contextualized by the expectation of liveness that comes both from the genre of sports and from the affordances of social media. To be a sports fan on social media is to be synchronously engaged, which happens easily online.

Social media also support the realness of sport. If the sports/media complex is built upon the assumption that fans get to see real events, that feeling is augmented by social media's apparently more direct access to the organizations and players. Sports social media are, therefore, a site in which parasocial relationships become particularly salient (Sanderson & Kassing, 2014). We saw earlier that the expectation of realness in Simple and Mass engagements of sports led fans to feel like they had a relationship with athletes and organizations, to the point that they self-identified with them (Coduto, 2022, p. 281). On social media, however, fans can interact with their object of fandom by following them and commenting on their posts (Sanderson, 2013, p. 57). Even the chance that an athlete or team account may engage with a fan through a like or comment increases the fan's feeling that the relationship is real. Because the more famous accounts will have millions of followers, it is unlikely that any particular fan will be lucky enough to interact with them. Still, it is the mere *possibility* that it could happen that validates and deepens the relationship. One-way relationships are a hallmark of parasocial relationships (Coduto, 2022, p. 282). Sports seem to reveal the real nature of athletes and organizations—an appearance only amplified through social media's parasociality. Therefore, digital sports fandom must be contextualized within the broader sports/media complex and the structures and meanings examined in earlier chapters.

Just as with sports industries and texts, sports fandom's connection to the generic conventions of sports are informed by hegemonic ideologies about race, class, gender, ability, and sexuality. That is, while digital media offer opportunities for resistance and equality, they are also sites for oppression and marginalization. For example, on college basketball message boards, it was found that fans used racialized interpretations of athlete disciplinary cases (Love & Hughey, 2014), and racism and Islamophobia flourished on soccer message boards (Cleland, 2014). Because digital media allow fans to comment on others' posts, they can police each other's posts for harmful messages. However, at least in the case of soccer fans on message boards, homophobic and sexist posts don't get contested by fellow fans (Kian et al., 2011). (Interestingly, in Jamie Cleland's (2014) study mentioned earlier, some fans in some circumstances would push back against discriminatory posts.) Even digital engagement that attempts to counteract hegemonic ideologies must be in dialogue with them (Hardin, 2014). The ideologies found within the sports/media complex's construction of the genre of live and real competition bleed into online sports fandoms.

Fan involvement with meanings common in the sports/media complex can be found in how fans interpret sports-specific phenomena. Sports texts often involve appraisal of the athletes' bodies (Chapter 2), which become an avenue for the expression of ideologies about race, gender, and sexuality. Fans, therefore, find themselves in a context in which these ways of understanding athletes are common and well understood. For this reason, we see "biological fandom" expressed in digital gaming, in which athletes are portrayed and viewed as biological commodities to be owned and exchanged (Mwaniki, 2017). We will consider the role that gaming specifically can play in biological fandom in the next chapter, but here it is important to note that fan engagement mirrors scripts common in the sports/media landscape. The sports/media complex portrays that the athletes' real value is demonstrated live during games, and fan engagement supports this notion.

Conclusion: The Blurred Nature of Live and Real Fandom

This chapter drew conceptual distinctions between kinds of fan expression and between the expression of the genre of sports in sports/media industries, texts, and fandom. These distinctions were made, however, only for conceptual clarity and not to suggest that there are significant boundaries between them. We know, for example, that the construction of the genre of sports occurs due to the interaction of industries, texts, *and* fandom; it isn't determined by only one source. It follows that fans aren't just monolithic passive recipients of the genre; they operate within it and help constitute it. As we saw, fans can resist and innovate, and fandom can be highly individualistic. This isn't to deny that the "production of meaning may operate within certain constraints, as few (if any) things are open to endless (re)interpretation" (Crawford, 2004, p. 118). However, fans have a significant role in establishing the genre of sports. They post on the Internet, call in to radio shows, and create a live atmosphere (Crawford, 2004, p. 3). Behaviors like these help construct live and real competition.

Furthermore, in some cases it is difficult to categorize whether an expression should be considered fan expression (and therefore covered in this chapter) or an aspect of the sports/media industries. For example, take "micro-industries," which are "small-scale versions of media production and distribution modeled after traditional forms of mass media" run by a small group of people or even an individual (Lopez, 2021b, p. 4). Fans involved in micro-industries could be studied from the lens of fandom, but it would also be appropriate to analyze their activities from an industrial perspective. Furthermore, fan activity regularly becomes conscripted by industrial and commercial logics. This happens saliently online when users—conceived of as "produsers"—help develop the product being sold, as with open-source software, *Wikipedia*, or *Second Life* (Bruns, 2008, p. 1). In sports, such conscripting often takes place when fans populate social media and blogging sites with posts (Johnson, 2021, p. 79). Activities like these are incredibly common; indeed, fans "are increasingly involved in the design and production of the sport experience" (Kennedy et al., 2022). While these fan behaviors can certainly be understood as self-expression and self-reflection, they also can be seen as work being done for sports media companies.

Just as the boundaries between the entities that build the genre are blurry, so too are the distinctions between the kinds of fans referenced earlier: Simple, Mass, and Diffused. Indeed, fans groups "may cross-cut all three audience types, even at the same instance, and furthermore this occurrence may be increasing" (Crawford,

2004, p. 25). Furthermore, there is good reason to think that sports companies are encouraging digital engagement both in stadia and at home (Clavio, 2013, p. 263). Given the affordances of mobile digital media, it is possible for fans to simultaneously be part of multiple audiences. A fan at a live event or watching from home, for example, can place a bet and post about it on social media. The mixing of audiences isn't exclusive to digital technologies; upon Vin Scully's death, many shared stories about bringing radios to live Dodger games so that they could hear his broadcast while watching in the stadium. These cases remind us that the lines drawn between kinds of audiences and what counts as fan behavior, while conceptually helpful, are not absolute.

The conceptual paring of fan performance offers a close analysis how fan roles and activities support and construct the generic conventions of sports. The particular modes of expression that are expected, encouraged, and afforded can be contextual, and thinking about those specific contexts helps demonstrate the nuances of generic expression. As we've seen, there can be differences in fan expressions whether they follow a game live in stadia, watch a television broadcast, stream it through a mobile application, or encounter social media updates. Furthermore, fans can engage with the genre and express their fandom in ways that are removed from the actual competition, such as by buying shoes, watching documentaries, and playing video games. The expression of fandom and its connection to the genre are particular to the context in which they occur.

However, approaching sports fandom as a broader concept also allows for an exploration of what the diverse fan performances share at their core. Fan identity articulation can indeed occur in different ways across many circumstances, but because their fandom is connected to sports, it is united by the genre of live and real competition. As we've seen, this doesn't always mean cheering at—or even watching—games. Rather, there are salient connotations associated with what it means to be a sports fan. Furthermore, all sorts of fandom involve consumptive and performative self-identification, and so the genre accounts for the sports-specific aspect of sports fandom. It is through identifying oneself with the conventions of live and real competition that accounts for the novelty of sports fandom.

Bibliography

Abercrombie, N. & Longhurst, B. (1998). *Audiences: A Sociological Theory of Performance and Imagination*. Sage.

Banet-Weiser, S. (2017). Brand. In L. Ouellette & J. Gray (Eds.), *Keywords for Media Studies* (pp. 24–27). New York University Press.

Billings, A. (2014). Reaction Time: Assessing the Record and Advancing a Future of Sports Media Scholarship. In A. Billings (Ed.), *Sports Media: Transformation, Integration, Consumption* (pp. 181–190). Routledge.

Bruns, A. (2008). *Blogs, Wikipedia, Second Life, and Beyond*. Peter Lang.

Clavio, G. (2013). Emerging Social Media and Applications in Sport. In P. Pedersen (Ed.), *Routledge Handbook of Sport Communication* (pp. 259–268). Routledge.

Cleland, J. (2014). Racism, Football Fans, and Online Message Boards: How Social Media Has Added a New Dimension to Racist Discourse in English Football. *Journal of Sport and Social Issues*, 38(5), 415–431.

Crawford, G. (2004). *Consuming Sport: Fans, Sport and Culture*. Routledge.

Coduto, K. (2022). Online Performances of Fandom: Selective Self-Presentation, Perceived Affordances, and Parasocial Interactions on Social Media. In D. Sarver Coombs & A. Osborne (Eds.), *Routledge Handbook of Sports Fans and Fandom* (pp. 273–284). Routledge.

Dimitrov, R. (2008). Gender Violence, Fan Activism and Public Relations in Sport: The Case of "Footy Fans Against Sexual Assault." *Public Relations Review*, 34, 90–98.

Georgiou, M. (2017). Identity. In L. Ouellette & J. Gray (Eds.), *Keywords for Media Studies* (pp. 94–97). New York University Press.

Guilianotti, R. (1999). *Football: A Sociology of the Global Game*. Polity.

Halverson, E. & Halverson, R. (2008). Fantasy Baseball: The Case for Competitive Fandom. *Games and Culture*, 3(3–4), 286–308.

Hardin, M. (2014). The Power of a Fragmented Collective: Radical Pluralist Feminism and Technologies of the Self in the Sports Blogosphere. In A. Billings (Ed.), *Sports Media: Transformation, Integration, Consumption* (pp. 40–60). Routledge.

Hills, M. (2017). Audiences. In L. Ouellette & J. Gray (Eds.), *Keywords for Media Studies* (pp. 17–21). New York University Press.

Jhally, S. (1989). Cultural Studies and the Sports/Media Complex. In L. Wenner (Ed.), *Media, Sports, & Society* (pp. 70–96). Sage.

Johnson, V. (2021). *Sports TV*. Routledge.

Kennedy, H., Gonzales, J. & Pegoraro, A. (2022). Digital Sports Fandom. In D. Sarver Coombs & A. Osborne (Eds.), *Routledge Handbook of Sports Fans and Fandom* (pp. 261–272). Routledge.

Kerwin, S. & Hoeber, L. (2022). Sport Fandom: The Complex of Performative Role Identities. In D. Sarver Coombs & A. Osborne (Eds.), *Routledge Handbook of Sports Fans and Fandom* (pp. 133–144). Routledge.

Kian, E., Clavio, G., Vincent, J. & Shaw, S. (2011). Homophobic and Sexist Yet Uncontested: Examining Football Fan Postings on Internet Message Boards. *Journal of Homosexuality*, 58(5), 680–699.

Kraszewski, J. (2008). Pittsburgh in Fort Worth: Football Bars, Sports Television, Sports Fandom, and the Management of Home. *Journal of Sport & Social Issues*, 32(2), 139–157.

Lopez, J. (2018). DraftKings: Daily Fantasy Sports Leagues, Legality, and Shifting Mobile Spaces. In J. Morris & S. Murray (Eds.), *Appified: Culture in the Age of Apps* (pp. 299–307). University of Michigan Press.

Lopez, L. (2021a). Excessively Asian: Crying, Crazy Rich Asians, and the Construction of Asian American Audiences. *Critical Studies in Media Communication*, 38(2), 141–154.

Lopez, L. (2021b). *Micro Media Industries: Hmong American Media Innovation in the Diaspora*. Rutgers University Press.

Lopez, J. (2022). ESPN+: Subscribing to Diversity, Marginalizing Women's Sports. In D. Johnson (Ed.), *From Networks to Netflix: A Guide to Changing Channels* (2nd ed.). (pp. 337–385). Routledge.

Lopez, L. & Lopez, J. (2017). Deploying Oppositional Fandoms: Activists' Use of Sports Fandom in the Redskins Controversy. In J. Gray, C. Sandvoss, & C. Harrington (Eds.), *Fandom: Identities and Communities in a Mediated World* (2nd ed., pp. 315–332). New York University Press.

Love, A. & Hughey, M. (2014). Out of Bounds? Racial Discourse on College Basketball Message Boards. *Ethnic and Racial Studies*, 38(6), 877–893.

Morris, J. & Elkins, E. (2015). There's a History for That: Apps and Mundane Software as Commodity. *The Fibreculture Journal*, 25, 62–87.

Mwaniki, M. (2017). Biological Fandom: Our Changing Relationship to Sport and the Bodies We Watch. *Communication & Sport*, 5(1), 49–68.

Parry, K. & Richards, J. (2022). Football Fans and Food: Feeding the Desire. In D. Sarver Coombs & A. Osborne (Eds.), *Routledge Handbook of Sports Fans and Fandom* (pp. 377–387). Routledge.

Sanderson, J. (2013). Social Media and Sport Communication. In P. Pedersen (Ed.), *Routledge Handbook of Sport Communication* (pp. 56–65). Routledge.

Sanderson, J. & Kassing, J. (2014). Tweets and Blogs: Transformative, Adversarial, and Integrative Developments in Sports Media. In A. Billings (Ed.), *Sports Media: Transformation, Integration, Consumption* (pp. 114–127). Routledge.

Sandvoss, C. (2003). *A Game of Two Halves: Football, Television and Globalization*. Routledge.

Theodoropoulou, V. (2007). The Anti-Fan Within the Fan: Awe and Envy in Sport Fandom. In J. Gray, C. Sandvoss, & C. Harrington (Eds.), *Fandom: Identities and Communities in a Mediated World* (pp. 316–327). New York University Press.

Wallace, C. (2018). Why "Black Panther" Is a Defining Moment for Black America. *NY Times.com*. www.nytimes.com/2018/02/12/magazine/why-black-panther-is-a-defining-moment-for-black-america.html.

Weed, M. (2007). The Pub as a Virtual Football Fandom Venue: An Alternate to "Being There?" *Soccer & Society*, 8(2–3), 399–414.

5
GAMES BASED ON LIVE AND REAL COMPETITION

This chapter examines sports games—games that are connected to some aspect of sports. Sport games include prediction games like fantasy sports, sports betting, and March Madness brackets; board games like *Strat-O-Matic*; video games like *NBA2k*, *MLB the Show*, and *Madden NFL*; and esports like the *NBA2k League*, *League of Legends* (*LoL*), and *Counter-Strike: Global Offensive* (*CS:GO*). As a whole, these games have different relationships to sports. Prediction games can be thought of as second-order games constructed around first-order sports. Second-order games involve forecasting the events of the epistemically uncertain first-order sports. Sports video games, however, operate separately from the first-order sports. The events that happen in the actual sports usually have little to do with the competition in the video game. It is certainly the case that the first-order sport is *reflected* in video games—part of their appeal is supposed to be that the games involve "real" players, teams, and stadia—but the game competition occurs in a bubble largely removed from the competitive results of the games of the first-order sport. The esports—organized video game tournaments—can involve sports video games like *NBA2k*, but they need not. For example, *LoL* is a 5-on-5 arena combat game of the fantasy genre, in which characters fight with spells and weapons like swords, axes, and bows. However, esports have occasionally followed more traditional sports in their organization of tournaments, coverage and broadcasts, and in-stadia experiences.

In the rest of this chapter, we will explore these games' relationship to the genre of sports. All of these games make use of the genre in particular ways. Prediction games depend on the epistemic uncertainty of live and real first-order sports and board games attempt to capture the strategy of sport competition. Sports video games are simulations (Stein, 2013; Kayali, 2013) or variations (Bogost, 2013) that reflect the liveness and realness of sports. Esports occasionally use

DOI: 10.4324/9781003164272-6

the generic conventions of traditional sports. Each of the following sections will be dedicated to how the particularities of each game reference the genre of sports.

The distinctions drawn between types of games based on live and real competition are not absolute and commonly borrow from and depend on each other. For example, the *NBA2k League* esport is obviously dependent on the *NBA2k* video game. Furthermore, both sports and non-sports video games use the mechanisms of prediction games, such as player drafts. So, while each section will highlight the novelty of how each game interacts with a particular aspect of the genre of sports, it will also be worthwhile to attend to the relationship between the three.

This chapter also synthesizes the work that has come previously in this book. The other chapters have explored how the genre of live and real competition is constructed and reflected in sports' and sports media's industries, athlete expression, representation, and fandom. Here, we will see how sports gaming retains similar connections to the genre, while opening up novel expressions through gaming conventions. Therefore—while each of the following sections will analyze the particularities of gaming—their focus will be on how the generic expressions of sport affect how these games are made and played.

It is important to note that games based on live and real competition aren't unique to sports. There has always been gaming based on other entertainment products; think particularly of Oscar pools in which participants guess who will win each category, and video games based on popular cartoons like *Pokémon* and *The Teenage Mutant Ninja Turtles*. However, for our purposes, it is the construction of the genre that is essential to games built around sports. In other words, through these games we can clearly see the expectation and assumption that "sports" are live and real competition. For example, betting on sports and fantasy sports both rely on the epistemic uncertainty of the real competition that gamers can watch unfold live. The genre is at work both in the mechanisms of the game and how it is sold to potential players. Sports video games attempt to capture the genre and encourage its players to think about sports in those terms. Similarly, esports appeal to the genre to generate and maintain fan interest. As the focus of the final chapter, sports games reflect the genre, as these games depend upon and try to capture the feelings of live and real competition.

Second-Order Sports Gaming

Playing second-order games based on first-order sports is as old as American first-order sports themselves. European, and especially British, colonizers brought their games of chance and sports, and re-established them as their time and resources would allow (Lang, 2016). Many of the structures and cultures in contemporary versions can be traced back to their second-order games. The most basic similarity is how second-order games are organized around the epistemic uncertainty of first-order sport. As unscripted competitions, the result of sporting events is never known with certainty until the end. Whether one wagers against a friend about the results of a quarter-mile horse race in the 1700s, fills out a March Madness bracket with coworkers, or makes a bet with the FanDuel Sportsbook that the Las Vegas Aces will win the WNBA championship, second-order games work only because the events of the first-order sport are epistemically opaque.

Epistemic uncertainty represents the most basic connection between second-order games and first-order sports' construction of live and real competition. While one can place a bet on a die roll or roulette wheel spin because those results are also unknown in advance, sports offers a particularly exciting entertainment product to base a game around. Other media have benefited from second-order gaming, each connecting with sports' intimate relationship to epistemic uncertainty: WWE wrestling pools, *The Bachelor* and *The Bachelorette* fantasy leagues, *Game of Thrones* deadpools. Even though the creators of these properties closely guard the events that have yet to be disclosed to audience members, everyone knows that many (in the case of wrestling) or all (*The Bachelor*, *The Bachelorette*, and *Game of Thrones*) of the details have been established before the events are seen.

Knowledge about the pre-established nature of these events, strictly speaking, has no effect on actually knowing the results of the events. Unless they are spoiled by someone watching in a different time zone or by a blogger like "Reality" Steve Carbone, the events are unknown by most of the audience. For the unspoiled fan, these entertainment products are just as epistemically uncertain as a sporting event, demonstrating the import of the construction of live and real competition in the sports/media complex. Though it might not differ experientially between engaging with other entertainment products, it still affects how sports are constructed, sold, and engaged with. Even though one could easily build an epistemically uncertain game around other entertainment products, the genre of sports as live and real competition sets expectations that make sports seem particularly well suited for second-order gaming.

As we've seen, protecting this aspect of sports is crucial industrially to keep it separate from other entertainment products, and we see this in the sports/media complex's usual relationship to sports gaming. Although it is more accurate to think of sports gaming as an essential part of the historical and contemporary sports/media complex, for our current purposes it is helpful to think of how sports leagues and media have related themselves to the games. In particular, sports leagues and media have historically positioned themselves ambivalently to second-order games.

From their origins in the early and middle twentieth century, sports leagues and teams have known that sports gaming is good for business. Gambling was a particular reason why games like football, basketball, baseball, and boxing became popular. Just as with horse racing before them, these sports profited from the interest and attention that gambling brought with it. Leagues, therefore, shaped their product to enable gaming by releasing information crucial to gamblers like starting players, injuries, and schedules, which allowed fans to gamble more regularly. Sports media followed suit by making this information available. Indeed, early sports organizations and media knew what has been proven in more contemporary contexts: games help create and deepen interest in sports (for research on how this is true for fantasy sports, see Karg & McDonald, 2011 and Randle & Nyland, 2008). For this reason, sports leagues and media companies have started to run their own games—like CBS's March Madness brackets and the English Premier League's fantasy game—to drive interest toward their properties, and have partnered with each other like the NBA and FanDuel.

However, this doesn't mean that the relationship between the sports/media complex and second-order games has always been and is currently a comfortable one. Because sports leagues base their brands around liveness and realness, any suggestion that the games aren't pure competitions is a serious problem. For example, "game fixing" occurs when a first-order game is altered by outside interests. Many cases involve bettors or bookmakers trying to influence the game according to their financial interests by bribing or threatening players, coaches, and referees. When fans (and other bettors) get the sense that games are being fixed, the sports' appeal will wane. This happened, for example, with early baseball; around the early 1900s competing baseball leagues attempted to stay in business by fighting off gambling scandals (Ginsburg, 1995). Sports leagues, therefore, must do everything they can to protect their brand and fight the impression that games aren't pure competition. Defensive strategies most often involve surveilling employees and imposing harsh punishments for transgressions involving betting. These policies are now in place in both collegiate and professional sports. However, the scope of the policies signals the leagues' ambivalence about gambling; as long as they advertise that their employees aren't fixing games, fans are consequently free to organize and partake in enjoying live and real competition through gambling.

Gamblers and bookies having an effect on the competition, however, is not the only kind of fixing. Furthermore, leagues and media might relate themselves to these other kinds differently. One version is called "tanking," which involves a team's ownership or staff deciding to lose games (most often) to obtain a better pick in the next year's player draft. Many leagues have set up a system, intended to increase parity, in which the worst teams have a higher chance at getting better draft picks—thereby distributing talent more evenly, in theory. In response, some teams will try to maneuver themselves into losing games to increase their chances of getting a good pick. They employ tactics like claiming to need to rest good players, starting inexperienced players to develop them, and sitting better players who could be considered to be injured. All these actions are fixing, as it is in the long-term interests of managers of a tanking team to lose first-order games, and so they make maneuvers outside of the game to lose more likely. Of course, these strategies are intended to win future games, but future interests are certainly altering the competition that is supposed to be live and real.

Despite the fact that both change the competition, gamblers fixing games is taken to be a danger and tanking is commonly thought of as appropriate managerial conduct. While leagues have instantiated rules to curtail tanking, teams still benefit from being closer to the bottom and it still is accepted as a normal part of the game. Fans might grumble about tanking, but the threat of fixing due to gambling cannot be tolerated by leagues. Tanking at least can be sold as teams trying to become competitive eventually. To see how it can even be branded, note the Philadelphia 76ers' claim that fans should "Trust the Process" of tanking for future success. By contrast, fixing due to gambling undercuts the leagues' framing themselves as live and real competition. Therefore, leagues historically have done everything they can to distance their competitive product from gambling and not tanking. Usually, major media companies followed suit and avoided focusing on gambling (Lopez, 2021).

However, recently, sports leagues and media companies have come to accept their connection to second-order games and gambling, and even encourage it by offering their own gaming opportunities. March Madness brackets and season-long fantasy sports demonstrate fan interest in gaming. When the Unlawful Internet Gambling Enforcement Act permitted online gambling on fantasy sports, Daily Fantasy Sports (DFS) were invented in response. DFS allows, as the name suggests, much faster play than season-long fantasy and therefore operates in a similar fashion to sports betting. The popularity of DFS paved the way for the normalization and eventual legalization of sports betting. Currently, major sports leagues and media companies sponsor with betting companies and openly discuss betting—neither of which would have been conceivable ten years ago. While being connected to sports betting and sports betting companies might shift fannish connections to sport (Lopez, 2022), it is an ambivalent or even profitable shift.

Sports leagues and media companies, therefore, are in a difficult position since they are trying to offer a product conducive to gaming and gambling while still retaining the feeling of epistemic uncertainty. On the one hand, their brands depend on the genre of live and real competition, which encourages second-order gaming and increases fan engagement. However, with these benefits comes the looming threat of fixing scandals that would undercut the brand's construction of the genre. This is why sports organizations and sports media have an ambivalent relationship to gambling and gaming; the sports/media complex does everything it can to promote fans' gaming while policing its employees to ensure that the second-order game doesn't appear to affect the first-order sport.

Sports Board Games

Second-order prediction games aren't the only kind of game organized around sport and therefore depend on its generic conventions. While the second-order games discussed earlier, like fantasy and sports betting, depend on the results of

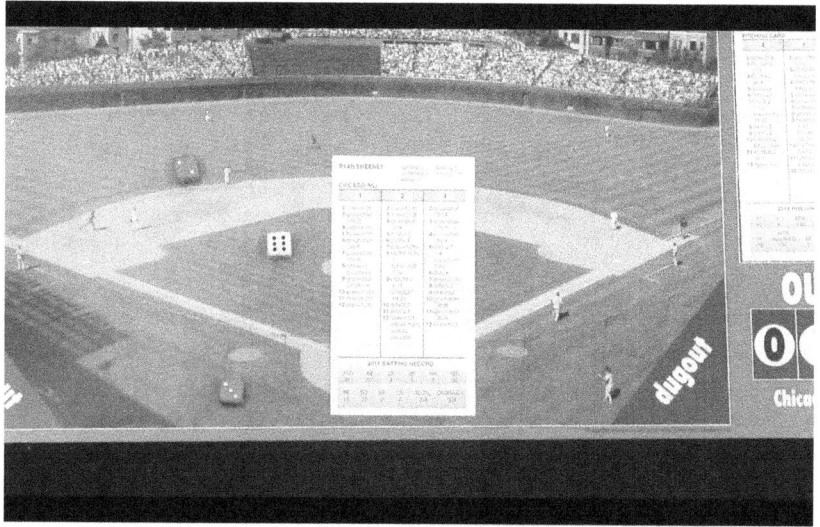

FIGURE 5.1 The main game components of *Strat-O-Matic Baseball*: a player card which reduces the athlete to a set of probable outcomes and dice which determine those outcomes during a game.

and events within first-order competitions, other games are more removed. Still, while one can play these games without engaging with the first-order competitions, they remain structured to benefit from their connections to the genre of sports. In particular, sports board games use gameplay mechanics to construct a way for gamers to play with the genre of live and real competition.

An early kind of fantasy sports game wasn't a second-order prediction game but a board game. In 1961, Hal Richman began selling *Strat-O-Matic*, a baseball-like board game based on MLB (Schwartz, 2004, p. 64). The game operated by encouraging players to think of themselves as baseball managers who make decisions like setting a batting lineup and choosing a starting pitcher. The baseball players were represented by cards that comprised probabilities of occurrences, like the odds batters will strike out, get a hit, or walk. Events were then determined by die rolls, which were connected to the probabilities on the cards (Figure 5.1). The game encouraged players to think of baseball players as a set of statistics, meaning gaming skill involved arranging a lineup that was most likely to win.

Games like *Strat-O-Matic* enable a kind of "competitive fandom" (Halverson & Halverson, 2008). In their study of season-long fantasy players, Halverson and Halverson (2008) examine how game structures enable gamer-fans to compete using knowledge of their object of fandom. The essential question for fantasy players is how they can use their understanding of first-order sports to overcome the epistemic uncertainty of future performances. *Strat-O-Matic* gaming works similarly, as a roster-building game that rewards fan knowledge. The principal difference between the two games is that *Strat-O-Matic* doesn't involve predicting the future performances of actual players. Instead, the primary source of epistemic uncertainty that is to be overcome is the randomness of the die rolls that determine the game's outcomes. Still, these games rely on the operationalization of fan knowledge by knowing how to build a successful roster to overcome unpredictability. While the gameplay of prediction-based fantasy is directly tied to the epistemic uncertainty of first-order sports (and therefore their generic conventions), *Strat-O-Matic* constructs a semblance of first-order uncertainty through the randomness of die rolls.

Which of these features are translated into the board game, and how they are translated, show which aspects of sports are thought to be desirable by those who make and play the game. In baseball board games, the primary focus is placed on the players and their interactions and, as with real-world baseball, highlights the struggle between pitchers and batters. While the results of the rolls are unknown in advance, the outcome of these conflicts is determined probabilistically based on the athletes' tendencies. Barry Bonds (a power hitter who many pitchers avoided throwing strikes to) is more likely to hit a home run or get a walk than the speedy Rickey Henderson (who is more likely to get a single than Bonds). The same logic works for pitchers; Nolan Ryan is more likely than the average pitcher to record a strikeout. Under the section titled "Baseball Realism," the rules state as follows:

> In Basic *Strat-O-Matic*, each batter is rated for his ability to reproduce his batting average and power, walks and strikeouts, how often he hits into double plays, and his overall fielding. He has separate ratings for his stolen bases and ability to take extra bases on his teammates' hits. Each pitcher is rated for how often he allows hits and walks, how often he strikes batters out, his fielding ability and his batting ability.
>
> (Strat-O-Matic *Baseball Rulebook, 2011, p. 1*)

Like a baseball manager, a successful *Strat-O-Matic* strategy involves knowing the roster of both teams and making pregame decisions about who is starting, which defensive position they'll play, and where in the batting order they will bat. The game directs attention to the players and their probabilities, such as knowing which batters fair better against right- or left-handed pitchers. Then *Strat-O-Matic* managers must make in-game strategy decisions based on game conditions and the opposing manager's strategy. For example, they might substitute a batter who is good at hitting left-handed pitchers when the other manager puts in a left-handed pitcher.

In these ways, board games reduce players to a set of probabilities that are supposed to correspond with their real-life counterparts. This conceptualization of the players as being true to life is core to the game; the first sentence of the introduction touts the game's "baseball realism and statistical accuracy" (*Strat-O-Matic* Baseball Rulebook, 2011, p. 1). To appeal to baseball fans, the game explicitly associates the realness of sports with statistically representing players. The relationship between baseball and statistical thinking has been around since the very origins of the game (Schwartz, 2004) and remains common in contemporary fandom (Burroughs, 2020) and broadcasts (Arth & Billings, 2021). Stats have been a common way to construct what happens on the baseball field and so it is easy for companies to use them to sell a game's representation of baseball.

The game, therefore, benefits from and helps support the notion of "biological fandom" in which the value of athletes is reduced to a biological analysis (Mwaniki, 2017). The bodily gaze is multifaceted and accounts for discussions of build, general health, and injury. In general, it involves reducing athletes to a set of stats that capture their worth (Mwaniki, 2017, p. 62). Games like this "are organized to reward deep knowledge of [athletes] as commodities to be acquired, traded, or discarded" (Oates, 2017, p. 130). This way of evaluating players is also found in coverage of sports, sports games, and fan cultures. It is, therefore, not just an eccentric baseball tradition that affords *Strat-O-Matic*'s selling itself through the connection between realism and probabilistic reasoning, but the wider sports and sports media context also encourage it.

We've already seen in that it is concerning to mix hegemonic ideologies with representation of liveness and realness, since those generic attributes validate ideologies (Chapter 2). This intermingling is particularly concerning in sports, since many popular leagues employ a labor force largely composed of people of color. Using statistics to determine people's value and usefulness can dehumanize athletes in a reductive way that seems scientifically and/or mathematically justified. Games like *Strat-O-Matic* use the apparent reality of stats to reduce players to a card of potential outcomes. They encourage game players to think of athletes as valuable or disposable according to their potential performance. Game players who thrive within this system must make decisions according to this logic. While players can engage in any sort of mindset and could decide to play skeptically, ironically, or even critically, the game's basic strategies and gameplay involve dehumanizing athletes.

Sports management games can also be played on the Internet. Baseball versions include *Sim League Baseball*, *Sim Dynasty*, and *Baseball Mogul*. There are management games for almost every popular sport: *Football Manager* (soccer), *Basketball GM*, and *Front Office Football* (American football). Management games encourage a season- or seasons-long perspective of a team owner, general manager (GM), or coach. *Strat-O-Matic* is not the only sports board game, or even the only baseball board game, but the game's structures and use of statistics to construct a notion of real gaming presaged the contemporary sports video games surveyed in the next two sections.

Sports Video Games as Management Games

Elements of sports management board games are now part of many kinds of contemporary sports video games. Indeed, games like *NBA2k*, *MLB the Show*, *Madden NFL*, and *FIFA* all feature a variety of ways to engage with and construct the sports genre. In these multimodal games, each mode can be organized on a spectrum between a management game (in which players make trades, select rosters, and assign lineups) and an in-game representation (in which players throw pitches, make passes, score goals, and shoot free throws). Players can choose to play these games as pure management games by making executive decisions or as pure in-game representations by simply playing the sport. However, most modes blend management and play decisions. Despite this, we will treat both components separately to analyze how they relate to the genre of live and real sports.

Just as with *Strat-O-Matic*, the primary game-based attributes of athletes are represented in a set of numerical categories. There are certainly aesthetic differences (like how the players are represented on-screen), and video game player skill can influence the digital athlete's performance. However, the differentiating factor between one athlete and another is how their attributes are rated. *Strat-O-Matic*, in this regard, has been particularly influential; the founder of EA Sports, Trip Hawkins, used *Strat-O-Matic* as inspiration for his video game company (Oates, 2017, p. 132) that now produces *FIFA* and *Madden*. It is common, however, for almost every major contemporary sports video game to share this connection with *Strat-O-Matic*. In *NBA2k*, players are rated on a host of attributes: Outside Scoring, Athleticism, Inside Scoring, Playmaking, Defending, and Rebounding. Each attribute has relevant subcategories with number values associated with them. For example, Inside Scoring contains Layup, Standing Dunk, Driving Dunk, Draw Foul, and Hands, all based on a 1–99 scale. *FIFA* works similarly but captures skills more relevant to soccer. They include 29 ratings, including Acceleration, Shot Power, Short Passing, Long Passing, Ball Control, and Heading Accuracy. Both games include mental attributes, like Pass IQ and Help Defense IQ for *NBA2k* and Composure and Aggression for *FIFA*. These rankings determine what actions the players are probabilistically capable of—much like the dice rolls and player cards of *Strat-O-Matic*. A good video gamer might be able to do more with an NBA player with a poor rating but that gamer would still be working against the player's rating.

Also like *Strat-O-Matic*, player rankings are supposed to reinforce the accuracy of the games and are used promote them (Oates, 2017, p. 137). This affords game designers the opportunity to sell a game as true to life, while creating hype. For instance, when the games are about to be released, their designers will often publicize their rankings. The result is often discussion (and sometimes outcry) by fans, sports commentators, and even the players themselves. Game producers encourage fervor by using advertisements and promotional videos with actual athletes

Games Based on Live and Real Competition 99

FIGURE 5.2 Cristiano Ronaldo holds the player ratings for his avatar during an advertisement for *FIFA*. Note, he has handwritten a "100" next to his actual "94" rating in the top left, performing his dissatisfaction with the rating.

reacting to their own ratings (Figure 5.2). The debates and conversations are always framed in terms of accuracy: Did the game get the rankings correct? Even disagreement occurs in the context of expecting the game to track reality and then falling short of that expectation or not. The games further add to this expectation by updating the ratings throughout the season in response to the athletes' actual in-game performances.

Sports video games use numerical systems to track the statistical view of the actual sports they are based on. The ratings for games like *FIFA* are constructed by data reviewers, who are "players tasked with monitoring the performance of athletes and encoding perceived changes onto the athletes' associated characters" (Srauy & Cheney-Lippold, 2019). Therefore, ratings are set through human judgment and within a social context. Srauy and Cheney-Lippold (2019) explore how data reviewers "reify racial biases into [*FIFA*] while shielding the game developers and themselves from critiques racism." They found that there was an "overrepresentation of black and Latino characters in physical ability and [an] underrepresentation in mental ability (and the inverse for whites)." The representation of athlete skill, therefore, ends up supporting racist tropes. Because the tropes are tied to the accuracy of the games, they are normalized as real. Therefore, *FIFA*, and the family of sports games to which it belongs, are sold based on more than just the realistic representation of the physical appearances of its athletes. They are also sold as aligning with social realism (Galloway, 2004). Games like these capture social realities and convey them back to the gamer. For example, if game players are led to think that Black players tend to be quicker or stronger than white players, they'll expect that from the game.

Player rankings undergird all these games' play modes. For example, in *MLB the Show*, players can decide to play a single game or guide a team through a post-season playoff run, an entire season, or even multiple seasons. For any of these modes, players can choose to play through individual games or choose to simulate portions of them. When the players compete in individual games, as noted earlier, ratings mark the conditions from which gamer skill can be exhibited. Simulated games, however, operate in a *Strat-O-Matic*-like fashion in which the ratings drive the probabilities of certain occurrences. That is to say, the ratings touch every aspect of sports video games; the effectiveness of lineups, using pinch hitters, bringing in relief pitchers, and trading players all depend on the ratings.

In some modes, the statistical view of the players is tied to fictional in-game currency and even (indirectly) to real money. Modes in which players take a more managerial role allow gamers to trade and sign players for in-game currency. The attachment of fictional money to players and their rankings encourages players to think about athletes' bio-value—the economic value of their bodies' capabilities (Mwaniki, 2017). In this sense, the values of the bodies of the athletes can be evaluated, bought, sold, and traded. All the games discussed here also have a mode in which actual monetary value is brought to bear: *MLB the Show* has Diamond Dynasty, *NBA2k* has MyTeam, and both *FIFA* and *Madden* have Ultimate Team. These modes marry the player ratings with a system that resembles a digital version of baseball card packs or collectible card games like *Magic the Gathering* (*MtG*) or the *Pokémon* trading card game. In those games, players can buy packs which have a random assortment of cards that are unknown by the player until they are bought and opened. Like baseball cards, both *MtG and Pokémon* cards are part of a market in which rarer cards are usually worth more money. However, the rarer *MtG* or *Pokémon* cards are also usually more powerful in the game. These video game modes borrow this component from card games like *MtG* or *Pokémon*; gamers may purchase digital packs with unknown game components, usually athletes, in which the rarer components are more potent in the game. Gamers can spend in-game currency to buy the packs, often called "loot boxes," and real-world money can be used to purchase the in-game currency. There are other ways to earn in-game currency like completing certain challenges but these gaming modes, therefore, have tied player rankings to an in-game economic system that can be influenced by real-world economic transactions. In this way, the rankings become tied to actual money.

Although not every gamer plays this mode and not everyone who plays the mode spends money, those who do so are encouraged to view the players as digital commodities whose worth is supposedly an accurate evaluation of their real-world value. That is, gamers can wonder whether the athletes are worth the money spent on them—not just the digital characters, but the athletes themselves, due to their alleged realistic ties to the digital characters. Through these games, players are introduced to a system of evaluating athletes as commodities, dehumanizing them using discourses of the objectivity of math and science born from competition. Such statistical ways to track the putative real worth of athletes are justified by (and justify) the realness of sports video games.

Sports Video Games as Simulations/Variants of Sports

Not only do sports video games construct a reality of what it means to manage a team, they also attempt to construct a reality of competition. *Madden NFL*, for example, promises on its website that it is "the most realistic digital football experience gaming has to offer" through "an immersive, simulation-based, authentic NFL interactive experience." Going beyond deciding who to start or trade, games like *Madden NFL* tell gamers that it is as close to playing on an actual NFL field as possible. Just as with the games' player ratings and management components, the claimed realness of the gameplay is a construction, and here it is based on watching sports broadcasts.

The most explicit way that sports video games appeal to reality is through their appearance. Even without touching a controller, someone could watch the video games and recognize that they strive to make the players, actions, and surroundings as lifelike as possible. The rosters of each team are made up by players that look like their real-life counterparts. Athletes even are occasionally invited into the game designers' headquarters to help them capture player-unique movement like a dribble, shot, or swing. All the gameplay happens on a court, pitch, or field that looks a lot like the actual competitive arena. The games' authenticity starts with how the sport is represented on the screen. However, what is the authentic experience being captured through the games' visualizations? That is, if the game is simulating the reality of a sport, what is the nature of that reality?

Sports video games don't exactly capture the experience of a particular on-field player, since they mostly show a camera perspective removed from any single athletes' view. *NBA2k* and *FIFA*, for example, take a side view of the court/pitch that is far enough away to see multiple players at once. A wide-frame view is helpful for gamers, as they need to quickly shift between controlling multiple athletes to play offense or defense. It is difficult to pass a ball, unless you can see where the open players are. It, therefore, is unsurprising that the view these games end up taking is more akin to the view of game broadcasts rather than the view of any one athlete. Both video games and broadcasts are aided by seeing more of the playing surface and multiple players. The video games' claim to reality is accordingly not based on capturing the players' experiences but instead rests upon broadcasts' claims to reality. *Madden*, for instance, takes a "view from the television booth" (Oates, 2017, p. 133). Even the name "Madden" is an eponymous reference to the player and coach-turned-broadcaster, and thus, a reference to televised games. If televisual broadcasts were thought to be manufactured constructions, then so too would the perspective of games like *NBA2k* and *FIFA*. But because we've already seen that broadcasts have historically constructed a notion of live and real competition, games based on those broadcast norms also associate themselves with the generic construction. Indeed, video games and televisual broadcasts together help construct what it means to watch and play live and real competition (Johnson, 2021, p. 74).

The connection between sports video games' construction of reality and sports broadcasts' construction of reality is revealed by the multitude of other ways the games attempt to capture the experience of controlling a broadcast game (Figure 5.3). Some ways add to the visuality of the game. The lucrative advertisements on the playing surface and player uniforms in game broadcasts are also shown in sports video games. It would, after all, seem odd to watch a modern English Premier League match or NBA game without being bombarded with ads, and so the games must also represent them. However, other components of the game replicate aspects of *watching* a broadcast game, not playing the game as an athlete or even being present in the stadium as a fan. These games often boast having famous announcers to comment on the game, which follow the usual sports broadcast convention of having a play-by-play announcer and "color commentator." Furthermore, just like in game broadcasts, natural breaks in the games—pausing for corner or goal kicks in soccer, timeouts in basketball, and halftimes for both—are supplemented

FIGURE 5.3   The primary view of *FIFA* attempts to capture the reality of a D1 Arkema match from the perspective of a televised broadcast.

with commentary, stats, and replays. Sports video games even add start-of-broadcast style introductions, in which player and game narratives are announced in a montage.

Other sports video games don't track the exact perspective of a game broadcast during gameplay. *MLB the Show*, for example, takes the broadcasts' usual perspective when the player is pitching (from behind the pitcher facing the batter), then during at-bats switches to a view behind the batter to see the pitcher. *Madden NFL*'s perspective, instead of being from the side—as football is usually represented during broadcasts—is positioned from behind the quarterback, with the length of the field running parallel to the viewer's perspective. Despite these camera angle changes to enable game play, the games still use all the constructions mentioned earlier to capture the reality of game broadcasts. Each still uses player likenesses and movement, accurate playing fields, advertisements, announcer commentary, replays, and montages. Furthermore, the behind-the-batter and behind-the-quarterback perspectives are now becoming common in televised game broadcasts. While they aren't the default way to capture a game, seeing a pitch, play, or highlight from those views is a familiar sight for fans of live broadcast sport.

It is worth noting that different modes of each game might offer a different perspective. Playing in Career Mode in *FIFA*, for example, allows a player to control a singular athlete rather than switch between the entire team over the course of the game. As the digital soccer player moves around, the game shifts the view on the pitch to follow the action. For example, if playing an offensive position, the field appears behind the team's goal facing their opponent. If, however, the player receives the ball running toward the opposition's goal, the view will zoom directly behind the player, giving a sense of an exciting breakaway. However, even though the mode doesn't replicate game broadcasts, it still looks, sounds, and feels like a game broadcast.

Sports video games are more than just an auditory and visual representation of a sport. They also construct a feeling that to play the game is akin to what it would be like to play the actual sport. This is no small feat, as holding a controller and pressing buttons is a very different experience from swinging a bat, dribbling a ball, or making a tackle. Furthermore, it is important not to conflate the difference between sports' rules and video games' mechanics. It is possible to scuff a baseball illegally to make pitching easier during an MLB game, which *MLB the Show*'s mechanics won't let the player do. Rather than be identical, games render playing a sport by reducing the skills of the sport to a set of discrete button options. *FIFA* offers basic options when your player has the ball: ground pass, lob pass, through pass, and shoot. These capture basic skills one might need when playing soccer on the pitch. However, button combinations diversify offensive possibilities in the game. A game player can also take a chip, finesse, or low shot; fake a shot or pass; make a driven ground pass, lofted ground pass, lofted through pass, or lobbed through pass. Just as with soccer played on the pitch, a game player's skills diversify and deepen as they practice and understand the game, giving the video game a sense of reality.

The game affords a similar depth and skill development when it comes to in-game strategies. We've already seen how the games afford managerial decisions. In *FIFA* these involve choices like which formation to organize one's team in, who to substitute in and out of the game, and whether to play aggressively or defensively. Sports video games also allow the player to make in-game strategic decisions that mirror those of athletes. For *NBA2k*, these decisions could involve deciding to run a pick and roll or to post up; for *MLB the Show*, which pitch to throw to a batter and where to throw it; and for *Madden NFL*, when to change from a pass play to a run or when to adjust a receiver's route. In these ways, sports video games mirror the in-game strategies of high-level sports athletes.

The similarity between in-game video game play and sports leads Ian Bogost (2013) to argue that sports video games are not merely simulations of sports but instead are sports variations. That is, he believes there are many ways to play a game like basketball; there are NBA games, WNBA games, both men's and women's college games, high school games, wheelchair games, recreation games, pickup games, three-on-three games, one-on-one games, pool games, and games of H-O-R-S-E. There is no single "correct" way to play basketball, or a reason to privilege one form over another. All these basketball variations have similarities and differences with each other in a Wittgensteinian family resemblance (2001). Sports video games, according to Bogost (2013), are also part of the category of sport; *NBA2k*, like three-on-three, NBA basketball, and H-O-R-S-E, is a variation of basketball. While some forms of basketball might be more similar because they involve shooting a physical ball into a physical basket (say, the NBA and H-O-R-S-E), others might be resemble each other because they share the detailed in-game strategy required by a 5-on-5 game (the NBA, WNBA, collegiate basketball, and *NBA2k*). This similarity of depth allows for high-level and even professional play in the NBA, WNBA, and *NBA2k* esport. The idea that sports games are variations of sports further reinforces their connection to the genre of sports; they do more than simulate live and real competition, they *are* live and real competition. Sports video games are structured to capture the novelties of sports—their strategies and in-game play—thereby representing a version of what it means to engage with live and real competition.

Esports as Live and Real Competition

Esports need not merely be variants or simulations of sports. While there are esports leagues based around leagues like the NBA and NFL, esports are broadly organized around "the player-versus-player competitions of the strategy, fighting, and first-person shoot communities and the player-versus-records of the speedrunning, high-scoring, and some MMO communities" (Boluk & Lemieux, 2017, p. 243). This section will consider esports broadly and therefore include leagues like the *NBA2k* League, *LoL*, and *Counter-Strike: Global Offensive* (*CS:GO*), regardless of whether they include an explicit connection to standard sports. The reasons for this will be discussed later: both conventional sports and esports are constructed in ways that make use of the genre of live and real competition. Due to the porous nature of the genre, sports can construct conventions alongside esports and even import them from esports.

There are profound similarities between the industries of esports and sports. Sports (as an entertainment product) matured alongside rule specification and institutionalization (Chapter 1), and esports followed a similar pattern (Taylor, 2012). Even though, in many cases, the rules of sports can be substituted for the video games mechanics—for example, a player can't make an illegal substitution in an *NBA2k* game because the game won't allow it—the norms around gaming are constantly being negotiated culturally and through ruling bodies (Taylor, 2012). For esports tournaments, this negotiation might involve regulating how a game is played beyond its mechanics, like allowed game settings or strategies, and how the tournament is run, like who is eligible to compete how teams are formed (Taylor, 2012, p. 63). Just as with sports, these rules and regulations provide the backdrop for live and real competition. They give the impression of a level-playing field from which athletes can fairly express their true abilities. Also as with sports, the feeling of pure competition that is aided by the notions of liveness and realness can come under attack through gambling scandals. We saw such attacks on liveness and realness in sports leagues, and they hold for esports leagues as well. As gambling scandals occur, confidence is lost in the leagues and players (Taylor, 2012, p. 82).

Furthermore, sports' focus on physicality adds to the association of live and real competition: sports captures bodies as they are doing the amazing feats necessary for high-level sports (Chapter 2). Similar themes are at work in esports, which focus on what the athletes' bodies are capable of: speed of actions, quickness in response, and coordination (Taylor, 2012, p. 38). These themes of physicality found throughout coverage conventions are similar to sports: game broadcasts, news coverage, gaming advice, and commercials. A survey of fan behavior reveals that fans of sports and esports engage similarly. Like sports fans, esports fans cheer, chant, and boo during live events and online discussions, engage with team sites, and follow news when away from the competition (Taylor, 2012). However, there are some differences between sports and esports fan engagement with a live and real competition. While we've seen that sports fans can identify with their object of fandom for all sorts of reasons, esports fandom can "divide along a number of different vectors" including "genre, a title, a player, a team, a national identification, and even in rare instances, a particular tournament" (Taylor, 2012, p. 190). A different set of identifications become salient because fans often play the video games that esport athletes also play.

Both sports media and video games construct a notion of reality. We've seen how this happens during coverage of competitive play in both realms, but it happens even at a more basic level of the design of the video game itself. In the earlier section, we considered how sports video games update their graphics to render them similar to game broadcasts. Another attempt at screen realism can also be found in the non-sports video games that esports are based on. *Call of Duty*, for example, is a first-person shooter that involves surroundings, weapons, and realistic characters that look as though they were taken from a movie set. In fact, famous actors occasionally star as characters in the game: *Game of Thrones*'s Kit Harrington, *House of Card*'s Kevin Spacey (before his sexual misconduct allegations), *Sons of Anarchy*'s Ron Perlman, and even Jeff Goldblum. The characters based on these famous actors look and sound like themselves in the game.

The attempt to attain a picture quality that rivals a game broadcast or movie is part of a wider attempt by video games to replicate sight (Boluk & Lemieux, 2017, p. 87). Such a replication is focused around a particular perspective; in particular, "perspectival rendering assumes that the position of the viewer is directly in front of and oriented toward the 'picture plane,' a two-dimensional field that typically coincides with the material surface of an image" (Boluk & Lemieux, 2017, p. 89). The fact that most games are oriented on a picture plane leads Boluk and Lemieux (2017) to conclude that "embodied vision is not properly perspectival but actually anamorphic" (pp. 90–91). That is, the reality of the games' appearance depends on taking a particular viewpoint. This is true even for games that don't feature realistic graphic representations of athletes, battlefields, or cities; even games like *LoL* and *StarCraft* assume this view. Whether following fantasy-like characters through a maze battle or building a base to war with other bases, the reality of game worlds depends on an anamorphic perspective, since they assume that the player is roughly in a position in front of the screen a few feet away.

Finally, video games also allow for player control and choice, which gives them a lifelike feeling. Players can try out strategies and play in ways that other media do not allow. As we saw earlier, video game options can be variations of real-life decisions; for example, sports games involve making managerial decisions. However, more fanciful games still involve controlling some component of the play. *CoD*'s choices involve where to go and how to defend and attack; *StarCraft* requires offense/defense and resource management; and *LoL* players control characters, their abilities, and their path through the game. Whether each game strives for realism or not, it parallels the decision-making that's part of non-gaming life, which feeds back into sports media broadly. As we saw, management decisions are a core component of sports board games and sports video games.

Furthermore, fans don't need gaming structures to highlight decision-making and choice in more typical forms of sports media. In a continually expanding sports media universe, fans can exercise choice about where to get their news, commentary, and games. For big events, some broadcasters have started to experiment with different feeds to attract fans with different interests. ESPN at one point offered a typical broadcast of an NBA game alongside a "MarvelCast" complete with Marvel characters. CBS covered an NFL Wild Card playoff game, while Nickelodeon aired it with references to popular cartoons. Choice is a hallmark of contemporary esports and the sports/media complex, allowing fans to navigate through its structures. Therefore, esports and the video games they are based on highlight both how sports' construction of liveness and realness can be applied to other contexts, and what other constructions of liveness and realness can reveal about sports. That is, the similarities between the constructions of liveness, realness, and competition offer a lens from which both can be examined.

Conclusion: The Magic Circle of Sports and Games

All the games surveyed earlier sell themselves by capturing one or more aspect of live and real competition. However, their connection to conventional sports can vary; they can be simulations or variations of sport or their connections to the genre of sport can be more implicit through industries, texts, and fan engagement. Since this is a book on sports media, sports have been foregrounded, but it is also worthwhile to think about the conceptual and ideological connections between games and sports more broadly. We have already explored how the liveness and realness of sports support and are supported by the notion of sports as a pure meritocracy (Chapter 2). Researchers on games have explored a similar notion that operates in both the sporting and gaming realms: the "magic circle."

Theorized by Johan Huizinga (2014), the magic circle is the concept that games create a "consecrated spot" (p. 10), in which usual norms are suspended during the game. This circle creates order, as "[i]nto an imperfect world and into the confusion of life is brings a temporary, a limited perfection" (Huizinga, 2014, p. 10). These ordered spaces include the boards of board games, the console and television of video games, and the field of a soccer pitch. The circle is temporary because eventually the play ends and the real world continues, meaning the play can also be interrupted or ended. One sort of interruption comes from spoilsports. They are not cheaters who pretend to keep the sanctity of the magic circle, instead they "rob play of its illusion" and therefore must be ejected from the game (Huizinga, 2014, pp. 11–12). Classic versions of being a spoilsport involve taking one's ball and going home or knocking over a board game before it is over, but also any non-game intrusion could count as spoiling.

While the magic circle is a helpful concept for theorizing about games and sports, it can be leveraged to do harm. In their discussion of the harassment of Anita Sarkeesian for exploring sexist tropes in video games, Stephanie Boluk and Patrick Lemieux (2017) found that the expectation that games created a magic circle were weaponized to censure Sarkeesian. Just as it was commonly thought that sports are apolitical and meritocratic realms immune from sexism, racism, and homophobia, Boluk and Lemieux note that Sarkeesian was treated as a "feminist killjoy" (Boluk & Lemieux, 2017, p. 283, citing Sarah Ahmed's 2010 concept)—a misogynistic version of being called a spoilsport. Because of her critique of the industry, Sarkeesian was critiqued for violating the sanctity of the magic circle:

> Aside from ad hominem attacks (which number in the hundreds of thousands), recurring comments continue to be published ad nauseam across all manner of social media platforms that work to reinforce and police the border of the magic circle of videogames. . . . These disavowals and dismissals of Sarkeesian's work are underwritten by the . . . magic circle that she was perceived not only as commenting upon or critiquing, but actively spoiling.
> *(Boluk & Lemieux, 2017, p. 283)*

These condemnations should ring familiar from our examination of athlete activism in Chapter 3; athletes are regularly attacked for violating the supposed magic circle of sports. Therefore, just as scholars of sport have done for the notion that sports are apolitical meritocracies, scholars of games have also routinely challenged the magic circle (Boluk & Lemieux, 2017, p. 282).

Magic circle ideals are so powerful around sports and games that they spill out from competition and into outside realms. This unfortunately happened to Sarkeesian, but it also happens to athletes when they speak up about social issues on their own time outside of the sports. Take for example, Laura Ingraham's claim that LeBron James should "shut up and dribble" after he and Kevin Durant discussed race and politics on an ESPN broadcast (Sullivan, 2018). Even the kneeling protests discussed in Chapter 3 occurred before the games and yet were still held to be violating the magic circle. This widening of the magic circle makes sense; as we've seen throughout this book, the genre of sports spreads far beyond the competition and is found throughout the sports/media complex in broadcasts, tweets, commercials, movies, and fan expectations. Every aspect of the complex that the genre touches is enveloped by the circle. For those committed to preserving the magic circle's alleged power, anything that sport or gaming touches is protected from critique. It is for this reason that a media critic like Sarkeesian got harassed for doing her job and that James and Durant were attacked for sharing their views. The genre of sport set the wide boundaries of the circle that were supposedly violated by intrusion.

Like the genre of sport, the magic circle is not politically neutral; it instead protects those in power. Therefore, claims of violating the circle are often reserved for those raising the concerns of marginalized groups. Indeed, both sports and games are rife with political and social messages, but those that are usually considered incursions violate, question, or even deviate from normal messages. The magic circle, whose scope is determined by the span of the genre, serves as a barrier to insulate anything associated with sports and gaming from certain political and social meanings. Not every sport, game, athlete, gamer, or fan participates in the magic circle to the same degree, but it remains part of the nature of sports' generic conventions. What is important for our purposes is that the genre of sports as live and real competition widens the magic circle to include non-sporting and non-gaming contexts, which is a thoroughly political and ideological phenomenon.

How the notion of live and real competition widens the diameter of the magic circle works similarly in both games and sports, and therefore we could think of them as closely connected. In a philosophical sense, all sports are games, but it is also possible to make the inverse claim that games share more with sports than might be obvious at first glance. Focusing on video games, Stephanie Boluk and Patrick Lemieux (2017) argue that the "perception of videogames as a sport is less of a philosophical question than a social, legal, and political issue with the most important factor contributing to the changing perceptions of competitive videogaming being the realization of its profitability" (p. 243). Their insight rings true for the connections between games and sports; as we saw earlier, the deep social, political, and economic similarities and insights about one helps us understand the other.

The porous nature of the genre of sports, and sports' connections to other types of entertainment, allows for exporting sports-based insights into other contexts as well as vice versa. For example, just as sports tell us things about games, so too can games tell us about sports. This is crucial to the conclusion of this book, in which we will focus not only on other contexts in which the generic conventions of liveness, realness, and competition are used but also what other genres of entertainment might tell us about sports. Since sports don't exist in a vacuum, we should expect that they are constantly in conversation with other genres like reality TV, game shows, and even scripted television.

Bibliography

Arth, Z. & Billings, A. (2021). Batting Average and Beyond: The Framing of Statistics Within Regional Major League Baseball Broadcasts. *International Journal of Sport Communication*, 14, 212–232.

Bogost, I. (2013). What Are Sports Videogames? In M. Consalvo, K. Mitgutsch, & A. Stein (Eds.), *Sports Videogames* (pp. 50–66). Routledge.

Boluk, S. & Lemieux, P. (2017). *Metagaming: Playing, Competing, Spectating, Cheating, Trading, Making, and Breaking Video Games*. University of Minnesota Press.

Burroughs, B. (2020). Statistics and Baseball Fandom: Sabermetric Infrastructure of Expertise. *Games and Culture*, 15(3), 248–265.

Galloway, A. (2004). Social Realism in Gaming. *Game Studies*, 4(1). http://www.gamestudies.org/0401/galloway/

Ginsburg, D. (1995). *The Fix Is In: A History of Baseball Gambling and Game Fixing Scandals*. McFarland & Company, Inc.

Halverson, E. & Halverson, R. (2008). Fantasy Baseball: The Case for Competitive Fandom. *Games and Culture*, 3(3–4), 286–308.

Huizinga, J. (2014). *Homo Ludens: A Study of the Play-Element in Culture*. Martino Publishing.

Johnson, V. (2021). *Sports TV*. Routledge.

Karg, A. & McDonald, H. (2011). Fantasy Sport Participation as a Complement to Traditional Sport Consumption. *Sport Management Review*, 14, 327–346.

Kayali F. (2013). Playing Ball: Fan Experiences in Basketball Videogames. In M. Consalvo, K. Mitgutsch, & A. Stein (Eds.), *Sports Videogames* (pp. 197–216). Routledge.

Lang, A. (2016). *Sports Betting and Bookmaking: An American History*. Rowman & Littlefield.

Lopez, J. (2021). Sports Betting and the Branded Purity of the Olympics. In D. Jackson, A. Bernstein, M. Butterworth, Y. Cho, D. Sarver, M. Devlin, & C. Onwumechili (Eds.), *Olympic and Paralympic Analysis 2020: Mega Events, Media, and the Politics of Sport* (p. 99). The Centre for Comparative Politics and Media Research.

Lopez, J. (2022). The Construction of Sports Fandom by Sports Betting Companies. In D. Sarver Coombs & A. Osborne (Eds.), *Routledge Handbook of Sports Fans and Fandom* (pp. 285–294). Routledge.

Mwaniki, M. (2017). Biological Fandom: Our Changing Relationship to Sport and the Bodies We Watch. *Communication & Sport*, 5(1), 49–68.

Oates, T. (2017). *Football and Manliness: An Unauthorized Account of the NFL*. University of Illinois Press.

Randle, Q. & Nyland, R. (2008). Participation in Internet Fantasy Sports Leagues and Mass Media Use. *Journal of Website Promotion*, 3(3–4), 143–152.

Schwartz, A. (2004). *The Numbers Game: Baseball's Lifelong Fascination with Statistics*. Thomas Dunne Books.

Srauy, S. & Cheney-Lippold, J. (2019). Realism in *FIFA*? How Social Realism Enabled Platformed Racism in a Video Game. *First Monday*, 24(6). https://firstmonday.org/ojs/index.php/fm/article/view/10091

Stein, A. (2013). Playing the Game on Television. In M. Consalvo, K. Mitgutsch, & A. Stein (Eds.), *Sports Videogames* (pp. 115–137). Routledge.

Strat-O-Matic Baseball Rulebook, (2011). *How to Play Strat-O-Matic Baseball*. Strat-O-Matic Game Company Inc.

Sullivan, E. (2018). Laura Ingraham Told LeBron James to Shut Up and Dribble; He Went to the Hoop. *NPR.org*. www.npr.org/sections/thetwo-way/2018/02/19/587097707/laura-ingraham-told-lebron-james-to-shutup-and-dribble-he-went-to-the-hoop.

Taylor, T. (2012). *Raising the Stakes: E-Sports and the Professionalization of Computer Gaming*. MIT Press.

Wittgenstein, L. (2001). *Philosophical Investigations*. Blackwell Publishing.

CONCLUSION

The Pervasiveness of Live and Real Competition

This book has made the case that the conventions and expectations of live and real competition have been developed in sporting contexts as a mediated entertainment product. With the contemporary popularization and reach of sports, it is worthwhile to consider how the generic markers have been exported. Indeed, sports have profited from being promoted as a novel entertainment experience, and so it makes sense that other media genres would borrow their conventions. This book will conclude with an exploration of how the genre of sports can be exported to other forms of entertainment. From game shows, to reality TV, and even to scripted television and movies, the conventions of live and real competition can be found throughout the modern media landscape.

Genre boundaries are porous, and any genre can reference any other genre. Focusing on televisual genres, David Rowe (2014) writes that, on the one hand,

> it can be proposed that television in general, especially in an era of threat to networked free-to-air broadcast delivery modes, is deeply reliant both on conventional sports contests, and on selected elements of them in other programming types in order to give them the "feel" of competitive uncertainty that is central to sports.
>
> (p. 100)

Sports' centrality based on its liveness and realness, however, does not mean it was insulated from other genres. Indeed, "mediated treatment of sports has also seen the importation of representational conventions familiar in other popular televisual genres, such as the melodramatic register of soap operas, and the scandalized tone of current affairs" (Rowe, 2014, p. 101). The popular genre of live and real competition expressed through sports, therefore, was informed by other genres. This concluding chapter will explore how sports shape and are shaped by other genres.

This book has highlighted the fact that the genre of sports is shaped across many different sites beyond on-screen narratives, and this applies to other genres (Mittell, 2004). Indeed, genres are constructed through industrial production and fan engagement as well (Mittell, 2004). An award show, for example, appeals to live and real competition through its televisual broadcasts by announcing winners in front of a studio audience, but its connection to liveness, realness, and competition also happens through journalistic coverage, advertisements, and social media commentary. Therefore, an analysis of the connection between the conventions of sports and other genres must involve more than textual analysis.

This conclusion will explore the connection the genre of sports has to other genres. The first two sections will examine game shows and reality television because they commonly reference live and real competition. They are, therefore, apt sites to explore how sports inform and are informed by other genres. The final section will turn to the very broad category of scripted entertainment. Scripted entertainment can involve a host of different genres, and they might have a weaker connection to liveness, realness, and competition than game shows and reality television. We will consider, however, how even scripted entertainment can borrow certain sports-like conventions in order to seem "of the moment" and to create hype. This book so far has made the case that the genre of live and real competition can be found uniquely across the sports/media complex, thereby arguing that there is something distinctive about the study of sports media. By concluding with an examination of sports' connection to other genres, sports media-focused research will be situated within the discipline of media and cultural studies.

Live and Real Game Shows

Game shows are incredibly diverse and, therefore, coming to a clear and distinct definition is difficult. Games like *Who Wants to Be a Millionaire* or *Jeopardy* test contestants' general knowledge since they can be asked about a wide swathe of topics. Some focus on niche knowledge, like *The Price is Right* and *Supermarket Sweep*, creating a game around the costs of goods like televisions and groceries. Other game shows are skill-focused, like the numerous cooking competition shows, or play up physicality, such as *American Gladiators*, *American Ninja Warrior*, and *The Titan Games*. Distinguishing between kinds of game shows with precision is difficult as many blend different categories; *Survivor*, *The Challenge*, and *Double Dare*, for example, all have their contestants compete in both physical and mental games. Even the genre of *game show* has fuzzy boundaries with other non-sport genres. For example, the aforementioned *Survivor* and *Challenge* have reality components. Popular shows like *Top Chef*, *Project Runway*, *RuPaul's Drag Race*, and even *The Bachelor/Bachelorette* franchise can be considered reality shows that follow a competition. Like all genres, the genre of game shows is fuzzy. Despite this, some sports-specific generalities can be found across game shows, and there are ways to organize some shows into sports-relevant kinds.

As the name suggests, game shows are constructed around a game. The competitive nature of each game can vary widely and, therefore, has varying similarities to sports and the expectation of physicality (Chapter 2). The stronger and most salient connections to sports can be found when game shows use the conventions of sports broadcasts. Sports' focus on bodies and what they are capable of is at the forefront of *American Ninja Warrior* and *The Titan Games*. These shows feature contestants prepping for the competition in vignettes, which often involve workout montages. The competition is shot from angles to follow its overall flow, but also makes use of close-up shots to highlight the contestants' struggle and emotions. Replays and slow motion are common, and these shows sound like sports. Crowds cheer on the contestants and announcers help make sense of the action. The latter convention has been borrowed from sports, even in game shows that don't focus on sports-like competition. *Iron Chef*, for example, has commentators help the viewer make sense of the competition while also informing them about cooking styles, ingredients, and techniques. *Battlebots*, as the name suggests, pits two robots in a ring to fight as announcers adopt sports announcers' tone and clichés. For games based on physical competition, all these conventions unite to elicit feelings associated with live and real competition. They riff on the excitement of not knowing what will come next, the spectacle of victory and defeat, and the drama of competitive, bodily conflict.

These feelings and associations from the shows are supported by promotional material, promising real and live competition. A 2022 video advertisement for *The Challenge: War of the Worlds* on Paramount+ starts with a *USA Today* quotation expressing that "*The Challenge* is America's 5th Sport." The ad then highlights "the biggest reality athletes" that will be competing against each other. There are shots of contestants running, climbing walls, and tackling each other often while shirtless (Figure 6.1). Muscular contestants are shown suspended and falling from heights, hanging off car roofs, and wrestling on top of a trailer being pulled by a truck. It is shot with many of the sporting conventions mentioned earlier.

Since genre is formed by more than the text, online commentary and coverage of the show promotes the idea that *The Challenge* is sport—or at least sport-like. The idea that the show is America's fifth sport can also be found on pop culture websites like Complex and Mashable, and sports/pop culture sites like Barstool and Grantland (Bill Simmons, the originator of the now-defunct site, claims he invented the phrase). *The Challenge* is also the subject of fan commentary on reddit.com and tumblr.com. The show's connections to the genre of sport are drawn in many different sites.

The genre of sports, as we've seen, involves more than just *physical* competition, and game shows can make use of those other conventions as well. Because

114 Conclusion

FIGURE 6.1 An advertisement for MTV's *The Challenge* as "America's 5th Sport" sells the show based on the physicality of its competitors.

sports are games, the construction of live and real competition available to sports, without reference to physicality, is also available to game shows. Yet most game shows are prerecorded and edited, so they don't automatically share the same feeling of the liveness of sports. There are exceptions to this, of course; *American Idol*, *Big Brother*, and *So You Think You Can Dance*, all mix prerecorded and live components throughout the season. Even shows without live segments, however, benefit from the convention of liveness. Due to the fact that game shows involve competition, they also are tied to the epistemic uncertainty of the events and results of the competition. Even though the game might be prerecorded, it remains connected to the assumption that the results of the competition were unknown at the time of recording. As long as spoilers are avoided, the uncertainty remains at the time of broadcasting for the wider audience.

The idea that liveness is tied to epistemic uncertainty also assumes that the competition is real. If people knew the results beforehand or could unfairly influence them, then the competition would lose its sense of purity. We saw this in Chapter 1, in which sports leagues did anything they could to retain the perception of fairness and therefore enacted severe policies against PED use and gambling. For example, being tarnished by assertions of gambling often leads to concerns that gamblers will pay players not to play their best so that the gamblers can profit from knowing the results in advance. Accusations of "fixing" harmed early eras of collegiate basketball, baseball, and boxing. Similar scandals occurred for quiz shows—a specific kind of game show—in the 1950s. Jason Mittell (2004) notes as follows:

> [I]n traditional accounts of the scandals, television audiences assumed certain generic conventions—such as "televised fair play" and "spontaneous unrehearsed competition"—as definitional elements of the genre [and] when the programs' actual production practices were revealed to contradict these conventions, the 1950s scandals ensued.
>
> *(p. 31)*

However, he notes that the story is more complex, as "skepticism about the genre's veracity was fairly common among commentators and audience members" (p. 36) and that the genre was also formed across other axes besides audience expectation (or lack thereof) like regulation and earlier radio shows. Just as with sports scandals, lines between what is considered "real" and "outside of the competition" are drawn beyond the text. Regulation and audience expectation form aspects of the genre like real competition.

Game shows and sports not only similarly make use of live and real competition, regardless of its perceived physicality, but they also share a similar approach to dramatizing competition. Sometimes, as we will see in the following section, foregrounding narrative elements that occur outside of the competition raises its dramatic stakes. This happens in shows like *The Challenge, So You Think You Can Dance, RuPaul's Drag Race*, and *Top Chef*. All these shows contextualize the contestants' competitive performance by foregrounding their personalities, stories, and interpersonal conflicts outside of the competitive dance stage, drag show, or kitchen. In this section, however, we will focus on the sports-like ways the competition itself is dramatized. Game shows like those named earlier regularly focus on the competition, while others—like *Jeopardy, Wheel of Fortune*, and *The Price is Right*—air only the competition. As noted earlier, many game shows are shot to emphasize physicality and epistemic uncertainty, thereby generating drama. Without the bodily focus, game shows that test people's knowledge still need to highlight the spectacle of competition using close-ups, stirring music, and markers of victory like confetti. The in-studio audiences also help instantiate the genre. While some shows subdue their audience, others take pains to rile them up. *The Price is Right* and *Let's Make a Deal* show enthusiastic audiences because contestants are chosen from who is in attendance. All game shows, however, use the audience to add to the drama and the feeling of liveness and realness in a sports-like fashion. In fact, for prerecorded shows, the audience even functions like a witness, attesting to the fact that the competition really unfolded live.

Competition has value when it seems live and real. There are, as we've seen, many ways to capture and construct this feeling. For that reason, competition can be found in many different contexts. Both sports and game shows similarly involve competition that can be used to generate excitement and pique interest, regardless of their other differences. It follows that both sports and game shows will continue to develop in conversation with each other and will continue to inform and formulate the genre of live and real competition.

Live and Real Reality Television

This section will consider how shows that don't include competition still make use of liveness and realness. An appropriate focus of analysis is the genre of reality television. When there is a lack of focus on competition, reality shows offer the opportunity to focus on the tropes of liveness and realness and how they are constructed. Reality television may or may not involve competition, but what is the genre? First, "reality TV draws upon other genres, including game shows, soap operas, dating shows, crime drama, talent shows, travel programs, and sports" (Mittell, 2004, p. 188). While it is helpful to note the breadth of what can count as reality television, its diversity also makes it difficult to define the genre based on content. For this reason, Jason Mittell (2004) argues that "the core unifying feature of reality TV as a genre is not any textual element, but the broad circulation of the reality TV generic label as a category, allowing us to make sense of these programs as their cultural associations" (p. 189). In other words, reality television "is a genre because we treat it as one, with regular iterations of the category in nearly every realm of media practice, from critics to networks, audiences to regulators" (Mittell, 2004, p. 189). Particular attention must be given to the formation of the genre by "producer, participant and audience practices" (Hill, 2015, p. 7). Across these, as the name suggests, there is an assumed tie to reality.

Realness is the major connection to sports, as it is recognized that sports could be considered the first reality genre (Serazio, 2019, p. 33; Sullivan, 2006, p. 131). Even without competition, the connections between the genre of sports and reality TV are robust. It is worth considering, however, how shows that do contain a competitive element draw on reality conventions to create interest and drama outside of the competition. As mentioned earlier, shows like *The Challenge*, *So You Think You Can Dance*, *RuPaul's Drag Race*, and *Top Chef* all portray a competition alongside what happens to the contestants beforehand and afterwards. Whether the noncompetitive events are depicted in a highly edited and musically driven vignette (as in *So You Think You Can Dance*), or in a 24-hour, fly-on-the-wall fashion (as in *The Challenge*), they are designed to increase the drama of the competition.

In many cases, dramatic amplification can be achieved by building "real" personal narratives. Reality shows will present the contestants' family, work life, preparations for the contest, pre-competition jitters, and post-competition reactions. These performances can elicit emotional reactions like sympathy or hostility, which increases engagement. Another common technique is highlighting interpersonal conflict. Conflict could not only generate like or dislike for contestants but also raise the stakes for the competitive narrative. Two contestants lip-syncing "for their life" in *RuPaul's Drag Race* or running headlong into each other during a "hall brawl" in *The Challenge*—dramatic events in their own rights—are made even more so when they are presented as the climax of an interpersonal conflict. Furthermore, these kinds of narratives are foregrounded in shows that don't draw clear boundaries between what is considered inside and outside of the competition. The contestants don't compete in a clearly delineated space (like a stage or kitchen) in *The Bachelor/Bachelorette* or *Big Brother*. When drama unfolds over who gets in-game rewards like a rose or a key, these shows blend competition and narrative to maximize dramatic appeal.

Even without competition, reality television retains the liveness and realness seen in the sports genre. We previously examined how a feeling of liveness is tied to epistemic uncertainty, even for shows that have been prerecorded and edited. However, some reality television is thought to be "of the moment" and part of the zeitgeist (Hill, 2015, p. 5). Its timeliness can be seen when shows are given the status of being appointment-viewing, and thus connected to sports mega events' status as being "zap proof" (Chapter 1). The idea that the shows are not to be missed marks their importance, which often is framed as being due to the shows' reflection of the current social moment; consider *American Idol* and the search for 15 minutes of fame, *Big Brother* and media surveillance, and *The Circle* quarantining participants to their living spaces during the COVID-19 pandemic. Although not every reality television show is so iconic, those that are especially popular gain a sense of liveness through the feeling of being an important part of the contemporary moment.

Reality television is connected to reality simply based on its name—but what specific conventions justify its name? Since much reality television is driven by the personalities of its participants, it is worth paying particular attention to how they are portrayed. It is generally acknowledged that reality TV stars perform for the camera (Hill, 2015, p. 53–63). It doesn't follow, however, that the genre doesn't benefit from the notion that *some* aspect of the "real person" is being represented. The "reality" of reality television, at least in this respect, falls between sports and entertainment like professional wrestling. That is, wrestlers might bring a small aspect of themselves into the ring but audiences don't expect them to act in-character during their out-of-ring life. Reality television operates in a similar way and promotes the expectation that there is *some* truth to participants' performances (Hill, 2015, pp. 53–63). It is common, for instance, for fans to get mad at the reality television stars themselves. If one is upset by Mike "The Situation" Sorrentino on *Jersey Shore* or Clayton Echard on *The Bachelor*, their ire is often focused on the person and not the portrayal of that person. Anger can also be directed toward actors in scripted entertainment—see Jack Gleeson's portrayal of

Joffery Baratheon in *Game of Thrones* and Anna Gunn's portrayal of Skyler White in *Breaking Bad*. However, emotions in reality television are elicited by a blend of on-screen and off-screen personalities. Fans don't think Gleeson acts like Joffery outside of the *Game of Thrones*, but the reality of reality television connects the participants' personalities inside and outside the show.

Despite the expectation of realness, the representation of reality television stars is a performance that involves the participants, producers, and audiences (Hill, 2015, p. 55). The construction of reality is akin to sports'; it isn't formed solely by the leagues, media makers, athletes, or fans. Instead, it is the result of a unified sports/media complex. Similarly, we can see the interaction of participant performance, production decisions, and audience engagement all forming the generic convention of reality. The previous study of sports media reminds us, however, that those who construct the genre go well beyond these three actors. The television channel or streaming service and their partners, for example, have a hand in formulating the genre too. Everything from when the program airs, how and where it is promoted, and who advertises with the show can help communicate that the show is a reality television show (Mittell, 2004). Hence, they all make a show more "real" than other kinds of television. Sports have given us the opportunity to formulate conventions of liveness and realness in order to study them in other circumstances.

Scripted Entertainment

The heterogeneity of reality television pales in comparison to the focus of this section: scripted entertainment. It would be impossible to cover all of the diversity in scripted entertainment in one section, let alone one book. This section invokes scripted shows to demonstrate that even non-live entertainment can make use of liveness, realness, and competition, and sometimes all working together. The most obvious connection is when scripted entertainment depicts some aspect of the sports/media complex, which was mentioned earlier as reflecting the genre of sports (Chapters 1 and 2). However, at this point in the book, it is worth focusing on cases in which competition isn't foregrounded. *Moneyball* and *Draft Day*, which were mentioned earlier, aren't focused on the athletic accomplishments of a sports team and instead spend more time on the actions of a sports teams' front office. While the performance of the team is relevant to the narrative, these movies revolve around player management and acquisition. Additionally, given the popularity of fantasy sports, it is unsurprising that a show developed around the game: *The League*. The show uses fantasy sports—including inside jokes and references to strategies (or the lack thereof)—as the organizing principle; it is the reason the characters interact. Despite that, these movies and show don't foreground athletic competition; they still are sports media because they engage with an aspect of the wider sports/media complex. As we've seen, whether running a team or a league, such actions make up sports media as both part of the sports/media complex *and* a portrayal of that complex. They represent what it's like to work in and play in that system, respectively. However, what about scripted entertainment that lacks a narrative connection to sports or competition?

In the remainder of this section, we will consider a few connections between sports and certain scripted entertainment, starting with the notion of appointment-viewing and mega events. In Chapter 1, we saw that sports are often taken as a hallmark example of both, partly due to the generic conventions of sports. There is value in being associated with a real competition playing out live, which means people will schedule time to watch the competition. That's especially true for mega events like the Super Bowl. However, the earlier study of game shows and reality television demonstrated that even recorded entertainment can retain a sense of liveness by being "of the moment" and "must-watch" events. If this can happen for prerecorded entertainment, it surely can for scripted entertainment.

Take *Game of Thrones* and *Breaking Bad*. Both shows were known for their unpredictability and drama. Major characters in both shows would betray their alliances, be betrayed, and even suddenly die. These shows' secrets were highly guarded before airing, as their narrative components generated similar drama and epistemic uncertainty to sports. They were taken to be appointment viewing and their final episodes were incredibly popular, highlighting the ways such shows leveraged uncertainty to become mega events. If even the apparently naturally live and real competition of sports is heavily manufactured to create these associations, versions of these maneuvers can be made available in other contexts. In fact, both *Game of Thrones* and *Breaking Bad* had a unique ability to draw on the conventions of sports. Both had gained a reputation of being prestige television with good writing, acting, and directing. Attracting a cult following and then widespread attention, they were perfectly positioned to make use of their sports-like appeal to uncertainty and drama to become appointment-viewing. Shows like these are reminders that generic formulation goes well beyond the text. They made use of sports-like industrial maneuvers and fan engagements, even though the narratives didn't revolve around any aspect of sport—putting aside the occasional joust or gladiatorial fight to the death. We can therefore examine the wider surround for other connections between sports and scripted entertainment.

Live and real competition offers many opportunities to drive engagement. When sports-like conventions are exported to other genres, they too can make use of sports-like gaming possibilities. It is common to organize games around the epistemic uncertainty of scripted entertainment. These games can involve trivia-style predictions in which players guess the events of the upcoming episode or season or highlight a particular narrative component of the show. For example, since *Game of Thrones* was known for killing off main characters in its large ensemble cast, the creation of deadpools—games in which players predict who lives and dies—became common (Figure 6.2).

FIGURE 6.2 *Super League Gaming* discusses strategy for a *Game of Thrones* deadpool, in which players select which characters will die in upcoming episodes.

We also saw in Chapter 5 that certain games purported to simulate the live and real competition of sports, and a similar effect can occur for scripted entertainment. Indeed, even shows and movies that don't involve competition can be turned into board and video games. Board games are particularly interesting, as they often insert player competition into a property that doesn't inherently have anything to do with competition, sports, or games. Take the *Battlestar Galactica* (*BSG*) board game, for instance. Aside from an occasional boxing match or pyramid game, *BSG*'s main plot doesn't involve sports and instead is a science fiction story, in which humanity tries to survive the genocidal attacks of sentient robots called Cylons. The franchise's reboot involves the plot twist that the robots, which are usually tall and metallic, can take human form and have been infiltrating human civilization for years. The game turns this narrative into a competition by casting each player as human or Cylon, with the Cylons starting the game pretending to be humans. The goal for the Cylons is to end the human race in show-specific ways like eliminating their food resources or destroying the titular Battlestar Galactica spaceship. Humans attempt to survive and find safety away from the Cylons. The game, therefore, takes the plot of the show and turns it into a competition.

Whereas sports games were built on their proximity to the sports they were representing, the authenticity of the *BSG* game depends on its connections to the show. Just as *Strat-O-Matic* allows players to pretend to be sports managers, the *BSG* board game encourages players to identify with humans fleeing genocidal attack or Cylons secretly sabotaging the human race. The game's competition makes playing it feel like experiencing the events of the show. Other board games similarly operate by distilling major themes and plot points of shows and movies into a competition. These types of games are reminders that sports are a valuable and unique form of entertainment, which have generated elements that can be found in non-sporting contexts. While we don't need sports to examine the structures of the games and their relationship to the show or movie they are based on, the study of sports can highlight the role that epistemic uncertainty or competition can play in constructing these games. This point also holds for the many ways that the genre of sports might be exported to scripted entertainment, even if they lack a connection to sports. For example, one could think about how the live audience of a sitcom operates like fans at a stadium to help generate excitement (McFall, 2014, p. 135). Thinking about how a studio audience elicits a sports-like sense of liveness and realness is analytically helpful. Sports are an enduring resource that, due to its widespread connections, can be used in these and many other future media analyses.

Conclusion: The Study of Live and Real Competition

The conventions of liveness, realness, and competition foregrounded in sports are found throughout the media landscape. The aforementioned chosen topics represent only a narrow slice of possible sites of analysis. For example, other focuses might include politics, and talk shows and news—all of which involve sports or sports-like constructions. The genre-specific conventions explored in this book offer a helpful starting point from which to conceptualize what drives their construction and effectiveness. Indeed, the analysis of sports media done so far charts many different ways that sports construct live and real competition, which then offers a road map for understanding their conventions in other contexts. The study of sports media is germinal in this respect. Not only are sports extremely popular but so too are genres of media that also describe themselves as immediate and authentic. Consequently, the study of sports media offers a helpful lens from which to analyze other kinds of media that don't even involve sports.

While this book is dedicated to making sense of the construction of the genre of sports, those of us who study sports media should continue to chart the particularities of sports media while simultaneously being cognizant of its multifaceted connections to media more broadly, and even its contradictions. Jason Mittell (2004) reminds us that "media genre analysis needs to recognize the role of contradiction and struggle within generic processes, looking to how generic categories operate primarily through the tensions arising from the cultural debates around genres and their role within media and society" (p. 44). We've seen that the sports/media complex uses live and real competition to set itself apart while simultaneously borrowing and being borrowed from other genres. This tension both justifies the study of sports media as its own subject of inquiry and legitimizes applying its analytical tools to the broader field of media and cultural studies. Sports offer a vantage point from which to see how common and powerful generic conventions of live and real competition are constructed. Doing so involves understanding not just the history of the genre and its current formulation at different sports media sites but also how it is reflected and constructed in other contexts and media genres. Sports media touch many aspects of the media universe and understanding the genre of live and real competition helps conceptualize its influential position in that universe.

Bibliography

Hill, A. (2015). *Reality TV*. Routledge.
McFall, T. (2014). *The (Peculiar) Economics of NCAA Basketball*. Palgrave Macmillan.
Mittell, J. (2004). Genre and Television: From Cop Shows to Cartoons in American Culture. Routledge.
Rowe, D. (2014). Sports Media: Beyond Broadcasting, Beyond Sports, Beyond Societies? In A. Billings (Ed.), *Sports Media: Transformation, Integration, Consumption* (pp. 94–113). Routledge.
Serazio, M. (2019). *The Power of Sports: Media and Spectacle in American Culture*. New York University Press.
Sullivan, D. (2006). Broadcast Television and the Game of Packaging Sports. In A. Raney & J. Bryant (Eds.), *Handbook of Sports and Media* (pp. 131–1146). Routledge.

INDEX

ABC Sports 24, 27, 29
Abdul-Jabbar, Kareem 58, 63
Abdul-Rauf, Mahmoud 58, 63
Abercrombie, Nicholas 75
ability 10, 12, 38, 49, 85, 99
accuracy: of representation 31, 60; in news 33; in games 97–100, 103
activism 71–73; as intrusion 9; mainstream visibility 58–59, 66–68; of Black athletes 63; in branding 64–66, 69
actors 59, 106, 117–18
advertising 81, 113–14, 118; athletes in 60, 98; to audiences 21, 48; commercials 26–27, 60, 81, 105; pervasiveness 26–27, 76, 102–03; *see also* Nike
affect 15, 76–79
Ali, Muhammad 51, 58, 63
Allen, Bruce 22
amateur sports 21, 29, 39–41
ambivalence 60–61, 92–94
American Idol 5, 113, 117
American Ninja Warrior 112–13
announcers: commentary 6, 26, 102–03, 113; PA 76, 80
Antetokounmpo, Giannis 54
anti-fandom 79
anti-racism 63–64, 66, 71
appointment-viewing 81, 117, 119–20
Arledge, Roone 24–25
Asian Americans 47, 79

athletes: as activists 63–72; behavior 18, 20, 31, 61–63; as commodities 42–43, 85, 97, 100–01; coverage of 22–23, 30–32, 42–45, 105; as labor force 16–17, 39, 58–62; performance 29, 79, 97–98, 105, 116, 118; politics of 9, 40–42, 69–71, 108–09; physicality 45, 48–49; *see also* Black athletes, bodies
audiences 72, 87; film 79; radio 24; taxonomy 75–76, 80–86, 95; television 27–28, 114–18, 121; white 19, 59, 61
authenticity: competition 5, 18, connection 15, 64; expression 59–60; ideology 8; games 101, 120

The Bachelor/Bachelorette 92, 112, 117
Banet-Weiser, Sarah 15, 66, 75
baseball 6, 50, 100; cheating 8, 18; coverage of 21, 23; gambling 92–93; Korean Baseball League 81; board games 95–97; *see also* Major League Baseball
basketball 7, 41, 49, 53, 97; G League 63; variations of 104
Battlestar Galactica 120–21
Bennett, James Gordon 21, 23
betting 8, 18, 22, 32, 91, 94; *see also* gambling
Big Brother 114, 117
Billings, Andrew 3, 30, 79, 97, 48
biological fandom 42–43, 85, 97

Black Lives Matter (BLM) 63, 65–70
Blackness: athletes 10, 19, 45, 48–49, 53, 69, 71; audiences 66, 79; masculinity 48, 61; representations of 54, 60–61, 63, 99–100; women 45
Blake, Jacob 68
board games 90, 94, 107, 120, 121
bodies 85, 105, 100, 113; evaluation of 9–10, 42, *43*, 44, 50; hierarchies 11, 38, 105; transgression 47, 49, 85
Bogost, Ian 90, 104
Boluk, Stephanie 106–09
boxing 21, 23, 27, 30, 50
branding 14–16, 34, 59–75; of ESPN 28–30; of institutions 18–20, 93–94; of media 31–32;
Breaking Bad 118–20
broadcasting 6, 23–28, 111, 113; access 2, 32–34, 64; basis for video games 101–105; mass 81–82; rights 5; realism in 106–108; simulcast 107
Brody, Evan 47
Butterworth, Michael 47, 52

cable 4, 28, 33–34
Call of Duty (CoD) 106
campaigns 61–62, 66–72
Carlos, John 58, 63
CBS 27, 32, 39, 40, 93, 107
celebrity 23–24, 32, 72; athletes as 3, 58–59, 63
The Challenge 112, 113–17
cheating 103, 105, 107
Chelsea 78
Cheney-Lippold, John 99
chronic traumatic encephalopathy (CTE) 19
class 21, 38, 41, 53–54, 78, 85
Cleveland Browns 78
coaches 31, 42, 69, 71
Cold War 51–53
college sports: baseball 114; basketball 28, 30, *40*, 44, 85, 114; boxing 114; football 16, 22–23; see also March Madness
commentary 25–26, 32, 34, 42, 103, 106, 112–15; commentators *20*, 24–25, 29, 42, 98, 115
commercials *see* advertising
companies: gaming 81, 94, 97; news 20–21, 32–34; sports 4, 15, 33, 50, 54, 87, 93
competition 5–12, 15–19, 28, 38, 50–54, 112–21; live and real 5–7, 12; pureness of 8–11, 20, 39–41, 54, 63, 93, 114; spaces of 38–39, 83, 107, 117
competitive fandom 95
concussions 19–20
conflict 21–22, 25, 117; *see also* opposition
constructs 2, 54, 121–122
consumerism 3, 27, 74, 80–82, 87; commodities 80, 85, 100–101
convergence 14, 33, 84
COVID-19 68, 117
Crossfit 45–*46*
CTE *see* chronic traumatic encephalopathy
cultural institutions 8, 10, 16, 18, 59, 66–71
Curtis, William B. 21

daily fantasy sports (DFS) *see* fantasy sports
De La Hoya, Oscar 48
deadpool 92, *119*–120
discourses 52, 65, 101; of purity 20
Disney 29, 75
documentaries 11, 29–32, 34
DraftKings 1, 81, 83
drama 113–20; from conflict 25, 28, 51; melodrama 7, 5, 31, 111; unscripted 28, 30, 113
Durant, Kevin 108

economic value 10, 39, 100
emotion *see* affect
English Premier League (EPL) *see* soccer
entertainment products 20, 58, 80, 105, 111–12
epistemic uncertainty 5; in events 16–17, 19; in opposition 51; in games 90–92, 94–96; in game shows 114–115; in scripted and reality television 117, 119–21
escapism 38, 41–42
ESPN 28–34; content 4, 11, *20*, *43*, 107–108; influence 15, 22; ESPN+ 31–33, 81, *83*
esports 2, 42, 90, 104–05, 107
ethnicity 48, 54, 71, 99
events 7, 16, 20, 26; pseudo-event 26; as "zap-proof" 26–27, 117
expectation 2, 5, 12, 15, 31, 115

fairness 8, 17–18, 38–41, 105
fan engagement 4, 8, 75–76, 82–83, 86, 112, 118, 120
fan performance 74, 77–78, 82–3, 86–87, 95–96

fandoms 28, 53, 74–77, 85–86; groups 78–82; *see also* anti-fandom, biological fandom, competitive fandom, oppositional fandom
fans 11, 27, 74–89; communities 67, 77–78, 84; of esports 105–107
fantasy sports 12, 18–19, 25, 32, 42–43, 83, 90–96, 118
femininity 44–45, 47, 49–50, 54
FIFA 98, *99*, 100–01, *102*, 103–04
first-order sports 90–96
Fischer, Mia 46
football 19–20, 25, 41, 49–50, 92, 97
Formula 1 50
Fox 26–27; Fox Sports 6, 60, *64*
Fox, Fallon 46
free speech 60, 62–63, 70

G League *see* basketball
gambling 17, 92–94, 105, 114
game fixing 93–94
Game of Thrones 92, 118, *119*, 20
game shows 111–13, 115–16, 119
games 97, 103, 106, 108–109, 120–21
Gantz, Walter 1
García, Justin 48
Garner, Eric 64
gaze 43–45, 97
gender 12, 17–18, 37–38, 52, 78, 85; discourses of 45, 47
genre: 3–5, 11, 33–34, 54, 86, 90–92; conventions 20, 27, 30–31, 72, 118–19; expectations 8, 12, 60, 75; markers 7, 15–16, 25, 75, 111; sports as 5–7, 37–38, 86, 109, 112
golf 42, 44, 50
Grantland 32, 113
Griner, Brittney 45, 49
gymnastics 41, 44, 47, 50

Halverson, Erica 74, 95
Halverson, Richard 74, 95
Hard Knocks 31
HBO 29–30
hegemony 7–11, 37–38, 44–50, 78, 85, 97
heterosexuality 47, 48
hierarchies 11–12, 18, 38, 43, 45–46
highlights *see* replays
Hills, Matt 75
hockey 25, 51
homophobia 48, 63, 71, 85, 108
horse racing 6–7, 21–22, 30, 92
Huizinga, Johan 107 *see also* magic circle

identification 11, 51, 74, 105
identity 67, 74, 77–79, 84, 105
ideology 27, 30, 40–45, 51–52, 107; constructs 7–12
immediacy 22–24, 84, 112, 121
inclusivity 47–49, 67, 78
Ingraham, Laura 108
Inspire Change see Let's Listen Together
intersectionality 18, 54
Islamophobia 85
Iverson, Allen 61

James, LeBron 7, 48, 63, *64*, 65, 108
Jeopardy 112, 115
Jordan, Michael 1, 11, 65
journalism: newsreels 22, 24; online 32–33; print 21–23, 28; sports 15, 20–28
journalists 6, 21–23, 27, 32, 42

Kaepernick, Colin 53, 58, 62, *64*–65
kneeling 9, 68–70, 108

labor 16–17, 60, 97, 68–69; *see also* athletes as labor
Latinos 99
League of Legends 1, 90, 106
leagues 16–21, 24, 32–34, 58–71, 92–94, 105
Lemieux, Patrick 106–109
Let's Listen Together 66, 68
Lin, Jeremy 47
liveness 5, 24–25, 27, 59, 81 in esports 105, 107; in reality television 116–19
LoL *see League of Legends*
Longhurst, Brian 75
Los Angeles Dodgers 77–78 80, 87

Madden NFL 98, 101, 100–104
magic circle 38, 41–42, 107–109
Major League Baseball 26, 47, 69, 77–78, 80
male gaze *see* gaze
management 10, 16–17, 31; games 42, 96–98, 120, *see also* video games
March Madness 32, 81, 93–94
Martin, Trayvon 63
Marvel 29, 107
masculinity 24, 44–45, 47–50, 61
McClearen, Jennifer 17, 46
media and cultural studies 1–2, 4, 112, 122
meritocracy 9–11, 41–42; as apolitical 63, 65–66, 68, 71, 107–08; discourses of 39–41

Mexican Americans 48
micro-industries 86
military 9, 52, 62, 69
Miracle on Ice 51–52
misogyny 18, 46
Mittell, Jason 3–4, 112, 115–16, 118, 121
MLB *see* Major League Baseball
MLB the Show 98, 100, 103–104
MNF see Monday Night Football
Monday Night Football 29, 32
movies 31, 51, 79, 111, 118
mundane software 83
Mwaniki, Munene 42–43, 100

Name, Image, and Likeness 40
narratives 4, 31, 52–52, 81, 116–120; *see also* scripts
NASCAR 2, 42
national anthem: performances before games 52–53, 80; protesting 9, 58, 64, 68–69
National Basketball Association (NBA) 14, 47, 54; and activism 63, *64*, 65–69; and Blackness 60–61
National Football League (NFL): activism in 60–69; safety 19–20; and ESPN 22, television 31–32, 107
nationalism 52–53
NBA *see* National Basketball Association
NBA Voices 66, 68
NBA2k 91, 98, 100–102, 104–105
NBC 20, 27, 31–32
NCAA 16, 28, 39
New York Yankees 39
Nike 7, 27, 48, 65
normativity 8, 49, 51, 108
NWSL *see* soccer

Oates, Thomas 19, 39–40, 43–44, 48–49, 97–98, 101
Olympics 31, 58; gender 18, 44, 47; nationalism 51–52
online 31–33, 84
opposition in sports 50–54
oppositional fandom 51, 79
othering 11, 18, 51–52, 75–78

Page 2 32
Paramount+ 32, 113
parasociality 85
parasports 10, 49
paratextuality 59
participatory 74

PBS 29–30
people of color 44, 47, 48, 69, 97
performance-enhancing drugs (PEDs) 8, 17–18, 114
performativity 80 82–83, 87
Philadelphia 76ers 94
physicality 2, 9, 10–11, 38, 42, 44–46, 49–50, 54, 99, 105, 113–114
Piazza, Mike 47
picture plane 106
place 38, 52–53, 77, 83
platforms 14–15, 28, 63
Pokémon 91, 100
police 9, 53, 67–69
policies *see* rules
policing 65–70
politics 9, 21, 52, 66–68, 108–109; apolitical as political 9, 41, 63, 65, 107–08
pool rooms 22–23
prediction 5, 90–91, 94–96, 120
prestige television 24, 29–30, 120
The Price is Right 112, 115
Pride of the Yankees 31
probability 95–96, 100
produsers 86
Pronger, Brian 38
Pulitzer, Joseph 21

queerness 45, 54–55

race 37–38, 44–45, 48, 52–54, 78
racism and racial justice 9, 20, 54, 59–63, 65–69, 85, 99, 107
radio 23, 24, 27–28, 33–34, 37
Rapinoe, Megan 58, 74
Real, Michael 5, 7
reality 5, 11–12, 18, 25, 33, 90
reality television 28–31, 59, 116–119
realness 5–8, 45, 116, 118; as a construct 18, 20, 58–59, 92, 106; in esports 105, 107
regionality 44, 52
replays 10, 25, 29, 81, 103, 113
representation 38, 47, 52 60, 65
Rice, Grantland 21, 32
Rise 54
rivalries 53, 78–79
Robinson, Jackie 69
Rome, Jim 24, 29
Ronaldo, Cristiano *99*
Rowe, David 3–4, 9, 27–28, 31–32, 34, 111
rules 17–20, 25, 115

Index

RuPaul's Drag Race 112, 115–17
Russell, Bill 58, 63

salaries 17, 39
Salute to Service 62
Santurio, Alicia 72
Sarkeesian, Anita 107–108
Say Their Stories 68
scandal 5, 8, 18–20, 93–94 115
Schefter, Adam 22
scripted entertainment 8, 16, 18, 112, 117–21
scripts 47, 49, 53, 54, 61, 86
Scully, Vin 87
second-order games 90–95
self-expression 75, 77, 84, 86–87
self-identity 64, 78–79, 82
Semenya, Caster 45
sensationalism 21
September 11, 2001 52
Serie A *see* soccer
sexism 20, 63, 85, 107
sexual assault 1, 61
sexuality 38, 44, 47–48, 78, 85
Simmons, Bill 32, 113
skating 41, 44, 50; *see also* hockey
slow motion *see* Replays
Smith, Tommie 58, 63
So You Think You Can Dance 114–116
soccer 32, 50, 53, 78, 85, 103, 107; Bundesliga 6, 31, 81; National Women's Soccer League (NWSL) 26, 32, 63, 65–66; Serie A 81; Union of European Football Associations (UEFA) 32; US Women's National Soccer Team (USWNT) 1, 58
social justice 9, 12, 53, 62–64, 66–68
social media 33–34, 64–65, 69, 83–87
Soviet Union 52–53
spectacle 9, 25, 27, 52–53, 113
spoilers 107, 114
spoilsports 107–108
sponsorship 60, 70
sports: as constructs 4–6; games 92, 97, 120; genres 15–16, 31, 34, 37, 59, 98, 117; history 28–30; media 3, 5, 7, 22, 33–34, 37, 76, 82–83 107, 118 121–22; media industries 12, 14, 37, 51, 74–75, 86, 120; pastime 7, 9, 30, 108–109, 116, 119–20; products 2, 49, 59, 91–92; venues 22–26, 76, 80, 82–84; *see also* competition, purity of; video games
Sports Illustrated 23

sports/media complex 34, 42–45, 84–86, 92–93, 118–19
SportsCenter 28–29
SportsCentury 30
Srauy, Sam 99
Star Wars 29, 31, 39, 79
statistics 25, 42–43 95, 97–101
Steinbrenner, George 39
stereotypes 10, 30, 54; *see also* tropes
Strat-O-Matic 95–98, 100, 120
strategies 23, 104, 106
streaming services 32, 81, 83, 87, 118
Suits, Brian 2–3, 38, 41
Super Bowl 7, 27, 68, 81, 119
Super League Gaming 119
surveillance 61, 71, 93
Survivor 5, 112
synchronicity 6, 10, 14, 58, 84

tanking 93–94
Taylor, Breonna 58, 68
technology 14, 23–24, 28, 83
telegraph 22–23, 28
television 3–4, 59, 72, 107; *see also* prestige television, reality television, scripted entertainment
television channels 4, 12, 28–29, 118
temporality 10, 117
tennis 44, 50, 62
Theodoropoulou, Vivi 53, 79
The Titan Games 112–13
Top Chef 112, 115–16
tournaments— 90
track and field 47
tradition 40
training camps 31
trans people 46
transmediation 4, 30
transphobia 18, 63
tropes 44, 47, 60, 107, 116
Trump, Donald 69–70

UEFA *see* Union of European Football Associations
UFC *see* Ultimate Fighting Championship
Ultimate Fighting Championship (UFC) 16–17, 32, 45, 50, 81
Union of European Football Associations (UEFA) *see* soccer
United States 52–54
unpredictability 16, 33, 119
unscripted content 5, 17, 28–29, 58
USWNT *see* soccer

value 10, 28, 43
values 11, 15, 29, 43, 84
Vargas, Fernando 48
video games 90–91; as management games 98–101; as simulations 101–107; as sport 109; *see also* broadcasting
Vogan, Travis 22–23, 27–32, 39–40

Washington Professional Football Team 22, 71
whiteness: audiences 19, 59; masculinity 45, 47–48; white supremacy 63

Women's National Basketball Association (WNBA) 10, 37, 58, 63, 65–66, 84
women's sports: coverage of 30, 44–46; governance 17; merit 54; physicality 49–50
World Series 26, 50
World Wrestling Entertainment, Inc (WWE) 2, 8, 92
wrestling 16–17, 117

X Games 34
xenophobia 18, 20

For Product Safety Concerns and Information please contact our EU representative GPSR@taylorandfrancis.com
Taylor & Francis Verlag GmbH, Kaufingerstraße 24, 80331 München, Germany

www.ingramcontent.com/pod-product-compliance
Lightning Source LLC
Chambersburg PA
CBHW051403290426
44108CB00015B/2142